Wilma George is Fellow and Tutor in
Zoology at Lady Margaret Hall and
Lecturer at Somerville College, Oxford.
She is the author of *Elementary Genetics,*
Animal Geography and *Biologist Philo-*
sopher: A Study of the Life and Writings
of A. R. Wallace.
Wilma George was visiting Professor of
Biology at the University of Oregon,
1962-1963.

ANIMALS AND MAPS

Also by Wilma George

ELEMENTARY GENETICS

ANIMAL GEOGRAPHY

BIOLOGIST PHILOSOPHER:
A STUDY OF THE LIFE AND WRITINGS OF
ALFRED RUSSEL WALLACE

Wilma George

FELLOW AND TUTOR IN ZOOLOGY
LADY MARGARET HALL, OXFORD

ANIMALS
AND MAPS

Preface by
Helen Wallis
SUPERINTENDENT OF THE MAP ROOM, BRITISH MUSEUM

UNIVERSITY OF CALIFORNIA PRESS
Berkeley & Los Angeles

University of California Press
Berkeley & Los Angeles, California

Library of Congress Catalogue Card No: 68–28808

Layout and design by Michael McGuinness

Printed in Great Britain by
Bookprint Limited, Crawley, Sussex

CONTENTS

ACKNOWLEDGMENTS

I am indebted to librarians and curators of museums in many countries who have brought out their books and maps for me but I owe particular thanks to Helen Wallis of the British Museum. She helped me to find new sources of information to support the thesis that animals portrayed on ancient maps are zoogeographically significant and she read critically through the completed manuscript.

I am grateful to the Principal and Fellows of Lady Margaret Hall for a grant from the Christine Burleson Fund towards the cost of research in the United States of America. I am grateful to the University of Oxford for a grant towards the cost of research photographs.

For permission to reproduce maps in their custody I am indebted to the Trustees of the British Museum London for figures 2.2, 2.5, 3.4, 3.6, 3.9, 3.10, 4.2, 4.4, 5.1, 5.2, 5.3, 5.5, 5.6, 5.7, 7.2, 7.3, 7.5, 7.8, 7.10, 7.15, 8.3 and 9.1; the Curators of the Bodleian Library Oxford for figures 3.3, 3.8, 4.3, 5.4, 6.2, 6.3, 6.5, 7.1, 7.6, 7.7, 7.9, 7.11, 8.2 and 8.4; the Bibliothèque Nationale Paris for figures 2.7, 3.2, 4.1, 6.1, 7.13, 8.1 and 9.3; the Biblioteca Apostolica Vaticana for figures 2.11, 2.12 and 10.1; the Dean and Chapter of Hereford Cathedral for figures 2.3 and 2.4; the Huntington Library California for figures 5.8 and 7.4; the New York Historical Society for figures 6.6 and 7.12; the Direktor of the Österreichische Nationalbibliothek Vienna for figures 6.4 and 9.4; the Trustees of the National Maritime Museum Greenwich for figure 3.7; the John Rylands Library Manchester for figure 3.5; the Trustees of the Mitchell Library Sydney for figure 9.4; the Biblioteca Estense Modena for figure 2.10; the Biblioteca Nazionale Firenze for figure 2.8; the Biblioteca Capitolo Vercelli for figure 2.6.

Finally, I wish to acknowledge Heinemann Educational Books for permission to reproduce figures 3.11, 5.9 and 7.14 from my book *Animal Geography*.

Wilma George

PREFACE

Mapmaking must have begun in the very remote ages of man's past. The first maps were probably simple route maps, for members of so-called primitive communities in the present day are found to possess an innate skill in drawing rough sketches of a limited area to show directions, distances, and relationships between places. This type of mapmaking predates the development of a written language. From such simple sketches, no more perhaps than a trace in the sand or cuts in the bark of a tree, more elaborate route maps came to be made. Features along the route would be represented in perspective, as landmarks to guide the traveller, and so a route map became a regional map, showing local topography. The most famous of all early road maps is the Peutinger Table, a map of the military roads of the Roman Empire, drawn about AD 280 probably from a survey made for the Emperor Augustus in the first century AD. Completed *ca*. AD 500, it is now known in a copy of AD 1265. This map depicts, on a strip twenty-two feet long and one foot wide, the whole of the world as it was known to the Romans. On it are prominently marked roads, cities, towns and villages, watering places and temples. Natural features such as rivers, lakes, mountains and forests are indicated; and in the three great cities, Rome, Constantinople and Antioch sit three rulers, believed to represent the sons of Constantine, enthroned as symbols of a tripartite empire.

Another type of mapmaking was devised for purposes of delimiting property or territory. Traditionally, the invention of geometry and the development of the allied craft of land-surveying are said to have taken place in ancient Egypt, where the yearly flooding of the Nile obliterated land-marks and encouraged cadastral survey as a record of land-ownership. The only surviving example, other than plans of buildings and gardens, is a map of the Nubian gold-mines, drawn on a papyrus roll in about 1300 BC, and now preserved in Turin. It marks in red the gold-bearing basin east of Coptos, and shows in addition the main road, the temple of Ammon, and some houses. A similar form of cadastral survey developed in ancient Babylon, where plans of properties and towns were inscribed on clay tablets, a number of which survive, the earliest dating from 2000 BC. The recently discovered rock-drawings in the Val Camonica, Switzerland, if correctly dated as originating in the second millenium BC, rank as the most ancient of European maps. They also are a form of cadastral plan, recording fields and streams in the district of Bedolina near Capo di Ponte. Such maps were made as an expression of man's very basic instinct for territorial possession. The European estate plans of the seventeenth and eighteenth centuries, embellished with rich iconographic detail to flatter a landowner's pride of possession, and the great Renaissance maps of a sovereign's domains, may be regarded as descendants of the simple property surveys typical of ancient Egypt and Babylon.

These two classes of maps, the route map and the property survey, were made for practical purposes. When local plans or estates were enlarged into regional maps, and itineraries were fitted together to form a survey of a whole empire, these two types of mapmaking began to converge upon a third type, the mapping of the world. In this evolution there was no orderly sequence, no simple progression from local to regional mapping, and from regional mapping to the world survey. Philosophers, not geometers nor land measurers, were the first to make maps of the world, constructed partly from personal experience and observation and partly from information available at secondhand. In their speculations on the nature of the earth and of the universe, it was natural that they should turn to some form of graphic portrayal. The earliest map of the world is a Babylonian tablet of 500 BC showing the world as a flat circular disc, surrounded by the earthly ocean and the seven islands of Babylonian cosmography. The earth itself is shown as no more than the kingdom of Babylon, schematically portrayed. This is not unlike the Chinese depiction of the world as a great continental land comprising the kingdom of China with the lands and seas of the rest of the world squeezed round the margins, a form of map which was in vogue in China from the late sixteenth century until the eighteenth or even the early nineteenth century of the Christian era.

Inheriting the mathematical and cosmographical ideas of ancient Babylon, the Greeks were making, in the days of Herodotus of the fifth century BC, the same sort of schematic map, showing the earth as a circular plane with surrounding ocean. Agathemerus, in the second century AD, named Anaximander of Melitus, a disciple of Thales, as the first, early in the sixth century, to draw the inhabited world 'on a plate', as he described it. Such maps were derided by Herodotus, who claimed to have a better idea of the form of lands and seas. He set about establishing the correspondences and relationships of places, based on a concept of the symmetry of nature. Inaccurate although his ideas now appear, they represented a serious attempt at scientific compilation; and they show that sectional maps and itineraries were now being put together in the construction of a picture of the world. As the three Greek sciences of chorography, geography and cosmography became established as descriptive studies of the region, the earth and the universe, maps were made as graphic records of the knowledge so gained. Thus Aristophanes, in his comedy, *The Clouds*, produced in Athens in 423 BC, had a geometrical instrument brought on the stage 'to measure up land'; it was to measure not the allotment of land, but 'the whole world' and the accompanying map showed 'the circuit of all the earth'. The sphericity of the earth was first propounded by the Pythagorean school, and was publicised in the writings of Plato. Strabo recalls that Crates of the second century BC was the first to make a terrestrial globe. Knowledge of the sphericity of the world enabled geographical locations to be fitted into a geometrical framework. The arrangement of places along parallels and meridians expressed in the writings of Herodotus, together with the information in itineraries, provided a picture of the world which could be built up on mathematical principles. Men had now attained a consciousness of their physical environment beyond their personal experience, and they had the means of expressing it graphically by generalization. From this accumulated knowledge Claudius Ptolemy, in about AD 150, produced his great treatise, the *Cosmographia* or *Geographia,* the crowning achievement of Greek geography. With Ptolemy a new cartographic language was established, and when Ptolemy's *Cosmographia* was rediscovered in western Europe in the fifteenth century, his rules and directions became established cartographic practice from then until the present day. The world was depicted in a scientific framework, which with its degrees of latitude and longitude, left room for an unknown hemisphere. As new knowledge was gained, it was grafted into the framework of existing knowledge.

Roman cartography was in general less scientific and philosophical than the Greek, developing on practical lines as the tool of an imperial machine. The most famous Roman map was the *Orbis Terrarum*, a survey of the world by M. Vipsanius Agrippa, made at the command of Agrippa's father-in-law, the Emperor Augustus, and completed in 12 BC. Known only from its description in the works of Pliny and others, it appears to have been a very detailed map, built up presumably from the Roman road itineraries, and it was probably circular in shape, thus differing from the Peutinger Table. Certain medieval maps, including the Hereford and the Ebstorf world maps, are now believed to derive from the *Orbis Terrarum* of Agrippa, and point to the existence of a series of maps now lost, which carried the traditions of Roman cartography into medieval Christian Europe. The small T-O maps popular in later Roman times may themselves have been derived from reductions of the Agrippa map, and these were the usual type of diagrammatic map of the world inserted in the geographical treatises of the period.

Medieval European cartography reflected the arrest and decline in geographical knowledge following the collapse of the Roman world. Ptolemy's *Cosmographia* remained known only to Byzantine scholars, and thence it came to influence the early students of Arabic geography. Only in one type of medieval Christian map does there survive, in very simple form, some concept of Greek geography. The hemispheric maps of Macrobius, drawn in Spain and later reproduced in the works of the Venerable Bede, Lambert of St. Omer and others, show the habitable world of the northern hemisphere and the un-inhabited world of the southern, marked with climatic zones derived from Ptolemy's 'clima', and they are orientated with north at the top. More typical as illustrations to monastic texts were the T-O maps of Roman origin, showing the 'terra habitabilis' of the Romans as a tripartite continental land mass. Asia, Europe, and Africa are divided by the Don, the Nile and the Mediterranean sea in the form of the letter 'T'. To conform with concepts of Christian cosmology, East was normally at the top, and Jerusalem at the centre. Some of the T-O maps were crude diagrams containing only the names of the continents, or, on Biblical authority, the names of the three sons of Noah between whom the world was divided. Others were drawn with pictorial detail, displaying, besides other features, the Garden of Eden as the terrestrial paradise in the Far East, and therefore at the top of the map. The 'Cotton' or 'Anglo-Saxon' map of the world, drawn in the 11th century, with its pillars of Hercules, and the 'Psalter' map of the late 13th century, with Adam and Eve separated by the Tree of Knowledge in the east, show how much detail could be incorporated into quite small maps. Other versions of the T-O were rectangular in shape, perhaps to denote the four corners of the earth referred to in the Bible. Such was the map drawn at the monastery of Silos at Burgos in AD 1109 to illustrate a copy of St. Beatus's Commentary on the Apocalypse, and expressing the ideas of the Christian Moors of Spain. Most elaborate of all were the great thirteenth century world maps preserved at Ebstorf and Hereford. The Ebstorf world map, now surviving only in copies, the original having been destroyed in the Second World War, measured 3·58 × 3·56 metres, although basically a T-O map with east as usual at the top. Now believed to have been the work of Gervase of Tilbury, an English teacher at Bologna, later a provost in Ebstorf, it provides an encyclopaedic picture of the world, incorporating in magnificent profusion information from current literary, mythological and geographical sources. The Hereford world map, 1·34 × 1·65 metres in size, was drawn by Richard of Haldingham, probably about 1290, and preserved as an altar piece in Hereford Cathedral. With its inscriptions relating to late Roman times of the late fourth and early fifth centuries, its references to the world map of Agrippa, and its extensive classical derivations, it is a remarkable example of the welding of two traditions. The framework of Roman geography has been modified in the light of Christian theology; east is at the top, Jerusalem at the centre, as in the normal T-O map, and a wealth of detail reflects popular medieval histories and bestiaries.

These medieval maps depicting Christian cosmology were predominantly the work of scribes in the scriptorium, and we know little of their methods of compilation. Limited although their personal experience might be, they were not closed to new ideas. The Crusades brought knowledge of western Asia to Europe, and the central place of Jerusalem on the world map was a natural expression of its importance in medieval Christendom. Many new place-names were added to the maps, as merchants, pilgrims, and crusaders ventured across the continents; but the new information could not be assimilated with scientific method. The surviving maps therefore appear as jigsaw puzzles of evidence from diverse sources, their underlying pattern discernible only after meticulous study.

The various schools of Islamic cartography proved more open to the spirit of scientific advance. In the first phase, they carried on the tradition of Ptolemy and other Greek scholars, so that al-Mas'ūdī in AD 947 could name the maps of Ptolemy and Marinus as two of the three best which he had seen. A native Islamic school emerged in the ninth and tenth century AD, producing first a geographical text, and then, in the following century, a stereotyped set of maps which was given the generic name of the *Atlas of Islam*. This comprised a map of the world and maps of the separate Islamic countries, constructed in geometrical and stylised form from itineraries, but modified by later geographers such as al-Bīrūnī (AD 1021). The Arabs were now travelling extensively in Asia and Europe, and in scientific knowledge and techniques they were moving in advance of Europe. The Norman conquests brought a further expansion of Islamic ideas, and under the patronage of King Roger II of Sicily (1097–1154) the great Arab geographer Idrisi produced two major atlases and descriptions of the world, *The Amusement of him who desires to traverse the Earth* in 1154, and *The Gardens of Humanity and the Amusement of the Soul* in 1161, a work which survives in a shortened version of 1192. These atlases, based on his own extensive travels and the itineraries available to him, mark the finest achievement of Arabic geography. They were superior to the cartography of medieval Christendom on account of the scientific method by which they were compiled and the wider field of knowledge upon which they drew.

The chief impetus to advance in western Europe in the later Middle Ages came through the evolution of a very different kind of map, the nautical chart. Designed to help mariners find their way at sea, it served a practical purpose akin to that of the road map, but it answered this purpose by depicting not the route itself, but coastlines and hazards to shipping. Sailors previously had relied on written itineraries which can be traced back to the *peripli* or coastal pilots of the classical world. Following the introduction of the mariner's compass in Europe towards the end of the thirteenth century, nautical or portolan charts were made as an extension of the *peripli*, constructed on a framework of radiating compass lines, and with north at the top. Places were marked round the coasts, and interiors were generally left blank. The earliest surviving map of this kind, probably of Genoese origin, is the *Carte Pisane* of the late thirteenth century; and northern Italy now became one of the two chief centres for chart making. The maps and atlases of the Genoese Vesconte illustrate the development of a systematic school. A second centre was in the Catalan kingdom at Majorca and Barcelona. The celebrated Catalan world map, 1375, by Abraham Cresques, Jewish cosmographer to the King of Aragon, marked a further notable advance. The nautical chart had hitherto been the very opposite of the theologian's map. It showed only known discovered coasts, and was normally limited to regions frequented by sailors, the Mediterranean, Black Sea, and north-west Europe. The introduction of Arabic geography to Spain brought a new impulse to cartography. Responding to the King's interest in the Far East, Cresques extended his chart to include Asia. He compiled his map both from current nautical sources and from the narratives of thirteenth and fourteenth century travellers in Asia—notably from Marco Polo's narrative. Continental interiors were filled with detail, and the map was thus a complete picture of the world as it was then known. Cresques showed Marco Polo crossing Asia in his caravan, Chambaleth, the city of the Grand Khan, and many features— physical and humanistic—in the broad belt across the Eurasian continent whence travellers on trading and religious missions had brought back reports. Outside these limits the author did not despise the more traditional features. Gog and Magog still inhabited the mountain-girt region of north-eastern Asia.

The Catalan map was the first of a series of maps which enlarged the range of nautical chart, and it can be regarded as the forerunner of the renaissance world map. When seamen and chartmakers such as Columbus began studying the medieval and renaissance textbooks to learn about the world beyond their experience, two schools of European cartography united in a single stream. The world map drawn in the monastery and the mariner's portolan chart alike became the tools of men projecting grand designs for the discovery of new routes to the East. Fra Mauro's world map, drawn in 1459 at Venice, was an enlarged circular 'mappa mundi' of traditional form, which gave one of the most detailed expositions of Marco Polo's Asia and also displayed recent Portuguese discoveries. Further, the rediscovery of Ptolemy's *Geographia*, which had been circulating in manuscript in western Europe since 1406, added a new perspective to cartography. Fra Mauro himself did not use Ptolemy's framework of latitude and longitude, and rightly declared Ptolemy's work out of date, but he took account of Ptolemaic geography, and he moved Jerusalem to its true position, west of centre in the Eurasian continent. Once Ptolemy's maps had been engraved on wood or copper to illustrate the printed volumes of the *Geographia* from 1477, they provided a widely accepted base map which could be corrected to incorporate recent discoveries. As the Portuguese advanced round the Cape of Good Hope, the land-locked Indian Ocean was opened out and Africa was made into a peninsula. The world maps of Henricus Martellus, *ca.* 1489 and 1490, show the Ptolemaic model adapted to the new knowledge, and one of these probably helped Columbus plan his voyage to find a western route to Asia. Further, the invention of printing from type and of engraving in copper and wood gave maps and atlases an accepted place in the libraries of educated men, and they were used also as handbooks and guides to merchants and statesmen. Thus almost immediately new discoveries became common knowledge and the talk of Europe. In 1494 the first printed representation of any part of the world appeared in the woodcut maps showing the *Santa Maria* in the Bahamas, included in the slender volume containing Columbus's famous letter *De insulis nuper inuentis*, first published in 1493. By 1500 a new continent had been added to the map. On the MS world chart of Juan de la Cosa, 1500, and of Caveri and Cantino, both *ca.* 1502, four of the five continents had taken shape, and in their iconographic detail conveyed something of the strange undreamt-of lands beyond the seas. The world map of Giovanni Contarini, 1506, was the first engraved map to show part of the American continent. The woodcut map of Waldseemüller, 1507, whence America acquired its name, was the first to show the new world as a continuous continent stretching from southern to northern hemisphere. In 1508 the first modern world map, by Johann Ruysch, was added to Ptolemy's *Geographia* (the Rome edition first published in 1478). This showed South America as the 'Mundus Novus' in a delineation similar to Contarini's. The twenty new maps added to the Ptolemy of 1513

designed by Waldseemüller formed the nucleus of a modern atlas,
and thus was a precursor of Abraham Ortelius's *Theatrum Orbis
Terrarum* of 1570. Running to many editions, this was in turn rivalled
by Gerard Mercator's *Atlas, sive Cosmographicae Meditationes de Fabrica
Mundi et Fabricati Figura*, completed in 1595, which introduced into
cartography the new term 'atlas' for a collection of maps designed
as such. By 1600 the five continents were established on the map.
The fifth was the great southern continent postulated by the theory
of balance between the land masses of the northern and southern
hemispheres, and attested by supposed discovery. The interior of the
continents were filled with rivers, mountains, forests, cities, towns and
animals culled from the reports of travellers, merchants, seamen
and explorers. Sebastian Cabot's engraved world map of 1544,
revised to 1549, gave Queen Elizabeth's courtiers in the Palace of
Whitehall a portrayal of the north-west passage to Asia through
Arctic seas, and (judging from the earlier edition) impressions of long
South American rivers, and of conquistadores fighting Indians in
Peru, along with other details derived from experience gained by
Cabot during his years of service first for England and then for
Spain. The beautiful MS atlas of Diogo Homem, made in 1558 for
Queen Mary and King Philip of England, provided a colourful
representation of the Portuguese and Spanish empires which monopo-
lised the rich tropical regions of the world. Sir Walter Raleigh was
drawn to the wild forests of Guiana in search of El Dorado by such
maps, perhaps by this very one. On the MS maps made by the Dieppe
school of hydrographers in the 1530s and 1540s the great peninsula
of the southern continent in the area of Australia was embellished
with scenes of animal and human life based on imagined discovery,
or perhaps from devious report through Portuguese contacts with
Indonesian peoples. Such maps proclaimed Raleigh's dictum: 'There
are stranger things to be seen in the world than are between London
and Staines'.

   A map may be regarded as an imitation of the world. As Donne
wrote in his *Valediction of Weeping*:

>   On a round ball
>   A workeman that hath copies by, can lay
>   An Europe, Afrique and an Asia
>   And quickly make that, which was nothing, *All*.

The various names once given to atlases, maps and geographical treatises, *Imago Mundi, Speculum Mundi,* the *Seaman's Mirror, The Theatre of the World,* emphasise the conscious imitative aspect of cartography which it shares with the visual arts. The history of map-making shows progress and change both in man's ideas about, and knowledge of, the physical environment, and side by side it displays changing techniques for depicting the environment. The maps which have survived from many ages and lands show certain common elements in the language of expression. The drawing of features in profile, the bird's eye view and the perspective drawing are natural devices to use. They are characteristic of early oriental and early American as well as early European cartography. We find in maps from these very diverse regions the caterpillar mountain range, the sugar-loaf mountain, trees outlined to represent forests, buildings and cities in silhouette against the sky-line. When the Spanish conquistadores under Cortes invaded Mexico they found the maps in the Aztec codexes comprehensible in their topographic features, although their inclusion of historical and genealogical data added to their complexity. The pictorial elements of almost universal currency enable the map user to see at a glance what is represented. No key to symbols is necessary, for they speak for themselves. Many geographical symbols of great antiquity are found in the Chinese language, and there is thus some parallelism between the evolution of cryptograms and the evolution of techniques in cartographic expression. Colour was used as an aid to pictorial representation, to make features more distinctive, and conventions developed in its use, related partly to the colours of nature and partly to preconceived ideas in cosmology developed from the philosophical concepts of the four elements, which as late as the seventeenth century gained allegorical representation on such maps as Frederick de Wit's *Nova Totius Terrarum Orbis, ca.* 1660. In medieval European maps the silhouettes of towns and often also the line of roads were marked in red, the natural waters, seas and rivers in green, and forests in grey or black. Some attempt at naturalistic imitation also explains the wavy lines for seas and rivers, and this was more strikingly displayed on Chinese and Japanese maps, through the influence of their schools of landscape painting. Some differences in signs adopted reflect differences in the environment itself. The road in medieval Europe, a visible feature on the landscape, was depicted by single or double lines. In pre-Columbian Mexican maps roads were indicated

as a row of footprints, and this symbol was also used to denote the
passing of time. Changing techniques in the reproduction of maps also
affected the use of symbols. The introduction of engraving in wood
and copper in Europe in the middle years of the fifteenth century and
earlier in the Orient meant that the cartographer was now concerned
with the production of his map in black and white, often leaving any
colouring to his assistants and to booksellers. Symbols became less
dependent on colour. Wavy lines for water or shaded coastlines took
the place of greens or blues for hydrographic features. It is significant
that the development of conventions to show the 'difference of places',
the tower and circle for example, was established by the Italian line
engravers in the fifteenth century, who adopted styles derived from
the miniaturist in his illumination of maps and charts. The conventions were then taken up and further developed in the German school
of wood engraving of the early sixteenth century. With improvements
in techniques of surveying, as well as of reproduction, mapmakers
began to introduce refinements, seeking to make more differentiation
between the sizes and orders of features. Signs became more sophisti-
cated and abstract, and needed a key for explanation. The earliest
map to carry a key appears to be Peter Apian's map of Franconia,
Das Francken Landt, engraved at Ingolstadt in 1533. The use of
symbols increased the range of depiction and enabled features to be
more accurately located.

It followed that in the sixteenth century cartography was developing in two opposite directions, becoming more ornamental and also
more exact. The exploration of new lands invited pictorial detail to
convey a vivid impression of the new world revealed. Thus the
renaissance world maps of Juan de la Cosa, *ca.* 1500, Cantino and
Caveri, *ca.* 1502, and those of the Dieppe school in the 1530s and 1540s
abounded in exotic colourful detail. The decorative arts in cartography reached their highest level with the great Dutch publishing
houses of the seventeenth century, the firms of Blaeu, Hondius and
Jansson. The magnificent baroque title pages of atlases, the title
cartouches, marginal views and other decorative devices on maps,
all conveyed a visual impression of the landscape, while the maps
themselves attained accuracy of detail, with features often shown in
plan rather than in profile.

This progression of cartography from the naïve drawings of the
traveller to the specialised work of the highly professional carto-

graphic workshop of seventeenth century Europe, reflected a growing comprehension of the physical environment, and improved
techniques in recording it. Among the features of the physical environment important to man birds and beasts have commanded a
special interest, as creatures closest to man, as a means of sustenance
to him, if domesticated, a source of companionship; in the wild, a
source of danger. Hence, when man began to depict the environment
in his drawings, animals were an inevitable feature of the scene. The
cave paintings at Lascaux and at Altamira depict the animals of the
chase. A narrative fresco in the Chien-Fo-Tung cave temples near
Tunhuang in Kansu, of the seventh century AD, shows men, animals
and landscape in a mural which is almost a map. (Panoramic maps had
long been an established tradition in early Chinese and Japanese
cartography, especially for coastal regions.) Animals of local hus-
bandry, the horse and deer, appear in the Bronze Age cadastral maps
of the Val Camonica in Europe. They were used very early as a form
of conventional sign. A Greek coin bearing a map of Messina, dated
ca. 500 BC, has a dolphin disporting itself in the bay, indicating the sea.

When travellers began to penetrate the distant regions of the earth
in the Middle Ages and later, they brought back to their homelands
both truly observed reports of the animals encountered and garbled
versions. The great discoveries of the fifteenth and sixteenth centuries
opened up huge territories with flora and fauna hitherto undreamt of.
Artists such as John White depicted the animals and fishes seen in
Raleigh's Virginia colony, 1585–1587, with a brilliant naturalism
and animals gained an accepted place in the iconography of the
continents.

Finally, with the beginnings of thematic cartography, animals
appear as symbols of their distributions on J. M. Korabinsky's
economic map of Hungary, 1697. It seems from this a logical step to
Heinrich Berghaus's *Physikalischer Atlas*, 1845, in which scientific
distribution maps of genera and species, showing the 'animal king-
doms' and 'provinces' with vertical diagrams to illustrate distribution
by height. The marginal illustrations of the animals themselves are
a striking feature of the English edition published by Alexander
Keith Johnston in 1848. Cartography had now a new vocabulary,
into which animals, men, and all natural phenomena with a spatial
significance could be fitted.

In the nineteenth century it was common to decry medieval maps as fanciful, a demonstration of man's ignorance in the Dark Ages of knowledge. Only recently has the geographical content of such maps been truly interpreted, its language read without expectation of a literal accuracy, to reveal a remarkable conspectus of knowledge. Similarly the animals and 'monsters' which adorn these and later maps reveal much zoological truth if they are studied with the eye of an expert. Wilma George has cast such an eye over the many maps on which animals have a place. She has contributed a major and original addition to the history of cartography in making scientific evaluation of map faunas. She shows that early maps provide data about the distribution of animals, and that knowledge of zoology is vital in interpreting the work of the early mapmaker. The embellishment of maps with animals was a valid part of the cartographic alphabet, to which *Animals and Maps* gives us the key.

I

Introduction

The history of mapmaking has attracted many authors so that most of the ancient maps have been accurately dated and satisfactorily attributed to particular explorers or to centres of scientific mapmaking. Much has been written on the accuracy of delineation, the increase in knowledge at different epochs and the generally attractive appearance of charts, maps and globes. In spite of this attention, historians and geographers have been content merely to observe that at some periods, or on some particular maps, much of the continental space has been filled with drawings of land animals and the oceans frequently filled with sea monsters. The geographer attributes this to the desire for decoration or to fill in otherwise blank spaces of unknown continents and usually dismisses 'those mythical monsters' without further comment.

Disregard of unfamiliar animals has a long tradition. John de Marignolli commented in 1334: 'and then poets have invented ypotamuscs and plenty of other monsters' (Yule 1866). Swift's well known quatrain finds a place repeatedly in the geography books.

> So Geographers in Afric-Maps
> With Savage-Pictures fill their Gaps;
> And o'er unhabitable Downs
> Place Elephants for want of Towns.

Curnow referred to this 'atrocious habit' as recently as 1930: 'The pictorial element can be carried to an extreme and in many medieval maps the symbols become so utterly pictorial that they were used not only to represent the known but also to mask the unknown'.

To what extent the animal symbols are 'utterly pictorial' seems never to have been studied. The possibility that elephants did, indeed, occupy land where there were no towns seems to have been overlooked. It seems never to have been accepted that the animals on many a famous map were neither fictitious in their form nor haphazardly placed round the world; that a detailed study of these 'symbols' through the centuries might reveal an entirely new facet of the map-maker's art.

ANIMALS

It is not fortuitous that some animals that occur in the Old World are missing from the New, that some animals are confined to one continent while others have a world wide distribution. Animals have come to occupy their present habitations as a result of their slow evolution and spread in the past. As the animals evolved, so did the outlines of the great land masses of the world. The reciprocal effects of animal evolution and land evolution have led to the character-istic distribution of animals round the world.

On the basis of its animals the world can be divided into six zoo-geographical regions which correspond roughly with the main con-tinents (fig 1.1). In the New World, the neotropical region corresponds roughly with South America and the nearctic region with North America. In the Old World, there are two tropical regions, the ethiopian occupying most of Africa and the oriental region stretching from south of the Himalayas to the Malay Archipelago. The Old World temperate zone of Eurasia is known as the palearctic region. Finally, there is the australian region corresponding to the continent of Australia with a few nearby islands.

Each region has animals peculiar to itself and each region has a

Fig 1.1 The zoogeographical regions of the world

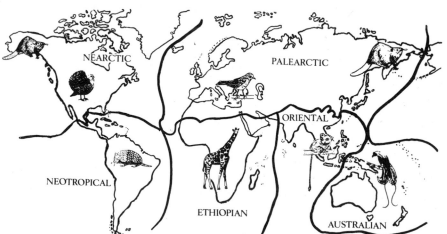

characteristic assemblage of the animals not so confined. Thus, there are no elephants in the New World, no opossums in the Old World, no bears in Africa and very few placental mammals in Australia. Instead, there are tapirs, armadillos and humming birds in the neotropical region; turkeys and beavers in the nearctic; beavers and hedgesparrows in the palearctic; ostriches, giraffes and rhinoceroses in the ethiopian; tapirs, rhinos and tarsiers in the oriental; and many families of marsupial mammals as well as egg-laying mammals (monotremes), cassowaries and birds of paradise in the australian region.

The early explorers setting out from Europe, from the Mediterranean basin in the early days, overland to China or across the seas to the New World in later centuries, would come across a fauna and flora whose composition would strike them as different from their own. Not only would they be unable to find some of the commoner mammals and birds with which they were familiar at home but also they would be struck by creatures and by plants they had never seen before nor ever heard of. From early accounts of travels and voyages, it is clear that men were aware of the strangeness of many of the animals they met. Further, they were interested enough to record them, often to describe them in detail and, in some cases, to bring home specimens or parts of specimens, such as the tail feathers of a macaw or a piece of prickly pear.

It is not, therefore, surprising that some of the cartographers, following the journals of expeditions or making their own observations on the spot, should have included as part of the land's features some of its peculiar animals, some of its plants. They were decorative but they were in all probability used diagnostically of the countries they inhabited, just as banners identified knights. If there were no towns to put on the maps, it is arguable that the animals or plants were as reputable an indication of the terrain as a range of hills or a river.

MAPS

Until 1477, when maps based on Ptolemy's *Geographia* were printed, there were only manuscript maps available. Some of these were made for generally instructive or decorative purposes: to hang behind an altar like the world map in Hereford Cathedral (fig 2.3); or to add to a nobleman's room like the Borgia map (fig 2.12). Others were the charts used by mariners. Others still were drawn to show advance in geographical knowledge. Comparatively few of these manuscript maps remain but they cover a considerable span of time from the Bronze Age to the sixteenth century. They are few in number until the fourteenth and fifteenth centuries. With the advent of printing, maps were being turned out in large numbers and copies of atlases and single maps from the sixteenth and seventeenth centuries survive and are readily available.

At all times, from the prehistoric to the eighteenth century, some maps have shown·more than coastlines. As knowledge of new lands increased so did knowledge of their natural products and these were frequently depicted on the maps. This is scarcely surprising since many early voyages were undertaken to exploit the natural products of far off lands. The quest for spices stimulated exploration of the far east, the fur trade developed from the discovery of the northern lands.

PLANTS

Plants occur freely on maps. Palm trees, for example, appear reasonably often in Africa: on the manuscript map of the Mediterranean by Jehuda ben Zara 1497 (fig 2.11) in the Vatican Library (Almagià 1948) and on the manuscript map of the world of 1550 by Desceliers in the British Museum. Palms occur in India on the thirteenth century Ebstorf map of the world (fig 9.1) in contrast to an oak in northern Asia. Some of the more unusual plants were slower to appear on maps. Cactuses, for instance, a spectacular order of plants and an order originally confined to the New World, are spasmodic in their appearance on maps; and yet many travellers to the New World had observed them and reported them in their journals. Pietro Martieri describing the new discoveries about 1525 (Eden 1555) reported cactuses in Hispaniola and Carletti reported them from Mexico and other parts of South America in his journal of his voyage round the world between 1594 and 1602. It has been suggested that the first piece of prickly pear was brought to the Mediterranean by Columbus. Cactuses appear on the South America of the maps in some editions of Peter Apian's *Cosmographia*, 1544 and 1584, for example; and, again, in 1710 in Allardt's *Atlas Major* (fig 3.10). But many of the plants are much less distinctive. Indeterminate trees appear on both sides of the Atlantic on the manuscript marine chart of Nicolo de Caveri of

1502 (Giraldi 1954) which is in the Bibliothèque Nationale in Paris (fig 3.1); and wisps of grass on the fragments of the Piri Re'is map of the world of 1513 preserved in Istanbul (Giraldi 1954). Many plants are of world wide occurrence and tropical countries show considerable similarities in their vegetation just as temperate regions share much of their flora. With outstanding exceptions, such as the cactuses, plants do not show clear cut localisation in the world. This is reflected in the records of plants on the maps.

MAP ANIMALS

In contrast, the localisation of animals was noticeable to the early explorers and clearly of interest to the mapmakers. For the most part it was the large animals, the mammals and birds with a few reptiles, that came to the notice of the explorers and were noted in their journals. It was these animals that found their way on to the maps. The tendency was mainly to stress the differences between the various parts of the world rather than the similarities and the abundant large animals provided a more striking contrast with home than insects and snails which must, however, have been much in evidence. As reports of new animals came to Europe the mapmakers recorded them in the new lands they drew on their maps.

Animals and Maps is the result of an investigation into the animals that appear on maps dating from the Bronze Age to the present day. It is the result of an inquiry into whether map animals are representative of real animals; into the extent that the animals reported by the early explorers found their way on to maps; into the correctness of the association of certain animals with certain continents; and into the change in knowledge of faunas between the time of the earliest cartographers and those of the eighteenth century. It is the result of asking whether the early cartographers were aware of the localisation of certain animals within certain continents whether, in fact, the maps were essays in zoogeography as well as geography.

Sea beasts have not been included. Like plants, their distribution is less restricted than that of many land mammals and birds.

Out of many hundreds of maps, globes and atlases that have been studied in the course of this inquiry some three hundred and fifty, dating from 1500 BC to AD 1804, were found to have significant animals on them. *Animals and Maps* is the outcome of the detailed study of the zoological content of these maps.

II

Ancient World & The Middle Ages

PRIMITIVE MAPS AND THE CLASSICAL TRADITION

The oldest known map of an inhabited site is a plan described recently from northern Italy (Blumer 1964). It is a plan of a village engraved on rock and dated at approximately 1500 BC, in the European Bronze Age. On the outskirts of the village are depicted a deer, cow, dog and donkeys, mules or horses.

The earliest known pictorial representations of the world were clay tablets made by the Babylonians (Unger 1937). A Babylonian cosmos of about 500 BC in the British Museum shows the central world of Babylon encircled by a fish-filled sea, with seven star points radiating from it and representing the seven islands of the world. To the west, island number three is represented by the drawing of a bird and described as being where 'the winged bird ends not his flight'. The seventh island lies opposite, in the east, and depicts the rising sun. The sixth, the next one north, has a drawing of a bull and is described as being 'where a horned bull dwells and attacks the newcomer'. Apart from this there are representational animals in the heavens but nothing else.

Although this early cosmos can hardly be called a zoogeographical map, it is interesting to find that some of the unknown distant parts of the world were characterised by the activities of animals.

From the early days of Greek and then Roman ascendancy in the science of geography few maps remain although undoubtedly there were both local itineraries and town plans as well as maps of the world. The geographers, on whose information many of the maps must have been based, were as assiduous in describing the fauna of parts of the world as they were in describing the direction of flow of a river or the curve of a coastline. Parts of southern Europe, India and northern Africa were sometimes known as districts from which certain animals came or which were deficient in what were considered common animals. Agatharchides Cnidius about 182 BC reported that elephants were found in India and Ethiopia but not in Libya (Müller 1855) and Strabo, writing between 7 BC and AD 19 was aware that 'some animals are to be found in India as in Aethiopia and Aegypt, and that the Indian rivers have all the other river animals except the hippopotamus' (Jones 1917).

Geographical theories could owe their origin to such observations. Several hundred years earlier Aristotle had suggested that 'one should not be too sure of the incredibility of the view of those who conceive that there is continuity between the parts about the pillars of Hercules and the parts about India, and that in this way the ocean is one. As further evidence in favour of this they quote the case of elephants, a species occurring in each of these extreme regions, suggesting that the common characteristics of these extremes is explained by their continuity' (Stocks 1930).

Military decisions could be taken as much on the presence or absence of animals as on the set of a river or mountain range. To Alexander, crocodiles meant the Nile. Strabo describes how 'when Alexander saw crocodiles in the Hydaspes and Aegyptian bears in the Acesines [Indian rivers], he thought he had found the sources of the Nile and thought of preparing a fleet for an expedition to Aegypt, thinking that he would sail as far as there by this river' a relapse into ignorance of animal distribution from the more accurate knowledge of Herodotus who knew that the Indus, like the Nile, is a river that has crocodiles.

There is little difference between this and the identification of the Gulf Stream by the absence of whales in its warm surface waters. A sea captain, Timothy Fodger, told Benjamin Franklin that 'we are well acquainted with the stream because in our pursuit of whales, which keep to the sides of it but are not met within it, we run along the side . . .' (Franklin 1786).

In spite of the importance attached to the fauna, the extant maps based on the geography of the time are mainly without illustrative animals. However, no Ptolemaic map is known from before the twelfth century so whether Ptolemy's original maps, if indeed he drew any, were devoid of animals or not may never be known.

Of the few maps that have survived from between the time of Ptolemy and the beginning of the twelfth century, a few depict animals. Fish in the sea are common but land animals less so. The earliest depiction of an animal on an extant map from this time, apart from decorative fish borders of some of the Beatus maps, seems to be the lion pursuing a gazelle across the plains of Moab on the Madaba mosaic map of about 560 (Bagrow 1964). The front of the lion is lost in a cloud of lion colour but the gazelle shows clearly its cloven feet and, with its short horns and short tail, looks remarkably like a Dorcas gazelle *Gazella dorcas*.

Four hundred years later on the Anglo-Saxon map of the world a lion again appears, in Asia. He is a splendid male lion and above him the inscription reads 'hic abundant leones' (Bagrow 1964).

Although these were only limited distribution maps, like the Babylonian cosmos, they marked a change, in that the animals were wild animals, accurately drawn and occurring in parts of the world where they were considered to be typical or even outstanding features of the fauna. Lions occurred abundantly in the near east and Europe until comparatively recent times, giving Xerxes trouble with his baggage camels as he travelled through Macedonia (Herodotus). A few lions still exist in India and the near east and there are gazelles in Arabia and into India.

T-O MAPS

In the early days of Greek mapmaking the earth was a disc with the oceans flowing round the edge (Raisz 1948) and, although Aristotle, Crates and Ptolemy favoured a spherical world, it was the disc map that continued with the Romans and influenced many of the medieval mapmakers. Agrippa, who died in 12 BC, was thought to have drawn an important map on this plan and the tradition was continued by, for instance, Saint Augustine of Hippo whose description of the world in Book 16 of *De Civitate Dei* 412–427 conforms exactly with a disc or T-O map.

T-O maps are so called because the O represents the boundary of the known world and within this the rivers Don and Nile form the horizontal stroke of the T and the Mediterranean the perpendicular, so that Europe occupies the bottom left segment, Africa the bottom right and Asia runs across the top (fig 2.1). Many maps of the Middle

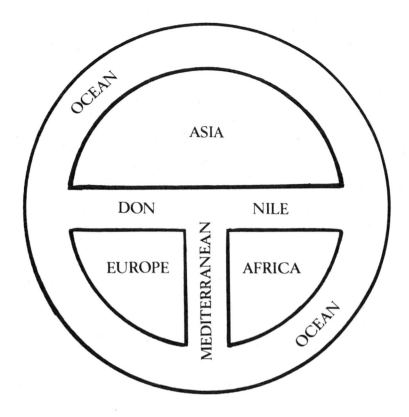

Fig 2.1 Diagram of a T-O map

Ages are of this pattern and so divide the world roughly into the three zoogeographical regions of the Old World: the palearctic region, the ethiopian region and the oriental region. To be more exact, the modern palearctic includes with Europe part of the Asia of the T-O maps.

Profusely illustrated are two of the best known medieval examples of T-O maps, the Ebstorf map (fig 9.1) of about 1235 attributed to Gervase of Tilbury and the Hereford map (fig 2.3) of about 1290 by Richard Haldingham (Miller 1895, Crone 1954, Bagrow 1964). On both these maps the animals vary in the accuracy with which they are drawn but, although at first glance some of them have the likenesses of animals that have never been, they are for the most part reasonable impressionist drawings of named animals.

On the Ebstorf map elkes, ures or aurochs the wild ox of Europe, bonacus probably the European bison, horse, alce mulo possibly the saiga antelope, two humped camel, lion, tiger and other large cats, bear, antdog, some snakes, a chameleon and the gryphe probably the golden eagle and other birds represent the palearctic region (though the antdog, saiga and chameleon are marginally in the oriental region).

In contrast an elephant, leopard, hyena, mirmicaleon, monkeys, camelopardalis, scarp, deer and tarandrius the reindeer with many types of snake, crocodiles, lizard and flying lizard, ostrich, ibis and other birds inhabit the ethiopian region (fig 2.2). The scarp is interpreted for not very obvious reasons as a giraffe by Miller 1895 but it seems more likely that it might be a misspelling of scart, nimble or quick, to describe one of the many African antelopes. The picture supports this interpretation.

The oriental region is less densely populated. There are fewer birds but there is a parrot. There are snakes, an antalops 'with long serrated horns, very difficult to approach', probably the blackbuck *Antilope cervicapra,* with long corkscrew horns, noted for its speed and still occurring abundantly in Asia, obvious to travellers and hunters because of its diurnal habits. The antdog, saiga and chameleon come marginally into this region. The saiga *Saiga tatarica* once swarmed over central Asia and its horns were much prized by the Chinese for medicinal purposes. It has the required proboscis-like upper lip: 'alce mulo similis superius habens labrum tam prominens ut pasci nequeat si non post terga recedat' as the Ebstorf map states. An inscription also announces the presence of snakes, tortoises, Indian bulls, unicorns, ibexes and the manticora but there are no pictures of them. Finally, there is an animal with one horn pointing forward and one backward. This is the eale or yale.

The yale which, according to this Ebstorf map, 'comes from India, has a body like that of a horse, the jaws of a goat, the tail of an elephant, horns a cubit in length, one of which can be reflected backwards as the other is presented forwards in attack, and which can move equally on water or on land'. This description on the map follows closely the original description of a yale by Pliny which was then copied by Solinus, about AD 250, through to the near contemporaries of the Ebstorf and Hereford mapmakers: for example, the author of *Semeiança del Mundo* about 1223 (Crowley and others 1959) and the authors of twelfth and thirteenth century bestiaries.

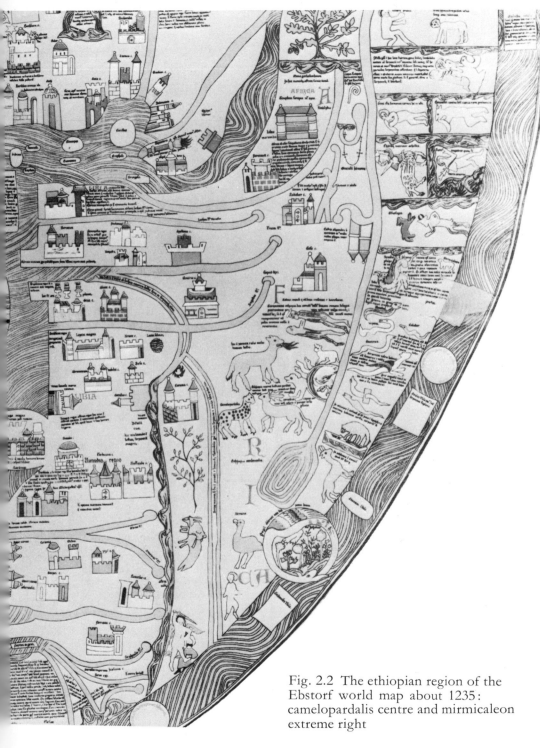

Fig. 2.2 The ethiopian region of the Ebstorf world map about 1235: camelopardalis centre and mirmicaleon extreme right

On the Hereford map there is also an eale in the oriental region with one horn pointing backwards and one forwards and the inscription is said to follow Solinus. It adds to the Ebstorf information that the eale is black, Pliny had said black or tawny, and that the horns are mobile. Both maps exclude Pliny's description of its being the size of a hippopotamus and neither of them has it looking in any way like one but they follow Solinus in thinking that its resemblance to a hippo is that it can take to the water as well as living on land.

The yale has usually been regarded as a mythical animal in the same category as the unicorn and argument has concerned itself lengthily with the problem of movable horns, one pointing backwards and one forwards. It is doubtful from the text whether Pliny meant any more by mobile than that the animal attacked first with one horn and then the other, turning its head. Solinus seems to have been the one to have introduced the notion of flexibility: 'for they are not stiff but are bowed as need shall require in fighting.'

There is no indication that either author thought the one horn pointed permanently backwards and the other forwards and this idea seems only to have come in later, with Vincent de Beauvais for instance.

In this context it is interesting to find that the eale in an Italian manuscript in Milan thought to be a copy of Solinus (Wittkower 1942) and a twelfth century bestiary eale in the Bodleian Library Oxford (MS 764) have long horns both pointing in the same direction. But other twelfth century bestiaries, in the British Museum (MS ADD 11283 and MS Royal 12 F xiii), have eales with one horn pointing backwards and one forwards and bear some resemblance to the Ebstorf and Hereford eales. In the bestiaries there was considerable confusion over whether the eale had jaws like a boar, with tusks, or like a goat, without tusks, but neither the Ebstorf nor the Hereford eales have tusks.

The animal that most closely fits the descriptions, but not necessarily the illustrations, seems to be the Indian water buffalo *Bubalus bubalis* (George 1968). It is a powerfully built animal, black, with swept back horns some two metres in length. It attacks with a sudden swipe of the horns which would account for the one horn at a time story. It lives in swampy ground or near rivers and wallows in mud holes.

The Hereford world map has many other similarities to the

Fig 2.3 Hereford map of the world about 1290 in Hereford Cathedral

Fig 2.4 Two humped camel in the land of Bactria on the Hereford map of the world about 1290 in Hereford Cathedral

Ebstorf map. In the palearctic there are again aurochs, bison, horse, two humped camel, tiger, other large cats, bear and golden eagles. The antdog, saiga and chameleon are absent. Monkey, genet and maneater are depicted for the first time in this region. There are pelicans, cranes and an ostrich in the Hereford palearctic.

The Hereford ethiopian region is characterised by fewer snakes and lizards than were found in the Ebstorf ethiopian region. There is no ostrich (which has migrated into the palearctic), no hyena, camelopardalis, elephant or mirmicaleon, although there are two gold-digging, insect-like formice. Instead, there is a rhinoceros and a monoceros.

Lizards are more prominent than snakes in the Hereford oriental. There are birds of which one may be an Indian hornbill, the so-called two headed bird. The elephant occurs here instead of in the ethiopian region, which is its home on the Ebstorf map. There is a crocodile and a wolf (marginally palearctic). The maneater, manticora, already noticed in the palearctic, is described in the inscription as living in India in spite of its actual siting on the map. And in writing it is referred to India on the Ebstorf map.

The maneater, manticor or martikora, had been described by Ktesias in about 400 BC: 'Its face is like a man's—it is about as big as a lion, and in colour red like cinnabar. It has three rows of teeth—ears like the human—eyes of a pale-blue like the human and a tail like that of the land scorpion, armed with a sting and more than a cubit long' (McCrindle 1882). This might be any of the large cats which vary considerably in colour and size from place to place or, more probably from the picture of it on the Hereford map, it might be a cheetah *Acinonyx jubatus*. Cheetahs used to be common throughout Asia. They have a rounded head, short ears, the pupil of the eye is round and the tail long. The claw, or sting, on the tip of the tail which has often been described for the large cats, seems to derive either from the distinct curl at the end of the normal tail or from the fact that the terminal vertebrae of the tail are often injured and displaced.

This interpretation is not dissimilar to that given during the second century by Pausanias: 'I am persuaded that it is no other than the tiger.' The preference for identifying it as a cheetah is strengthened by the fact that a tiger is represented next to the manticora on the Hereford map, although tiger was a name given generally to the large cats. The manticora of the map is described in much the same words as Ktesias used, with the additional information that it had a hissing voice. The tiger is described as being a very fast animal.

It would be hard to take exception to the placing of any of these animals all of which are representative of the parts of the world in which they occur with the exception of the deer in the ethiopian region, a monkey which unaccountably sits in Norway and the northerly placing of the ostrich on the Hereford map. It might also be argued that elephants should have equally occurred in the ethiopian region and rhinoceroses in the oriental if they were to be depicted at all but this seems to be too demanding. What is remarkable is that at this time the positioning of the animals chosen for record should be so adequate and based presumably only on the accounts of the classical writers from Herodotus to Pliny, Aelian and Isidore of Seville, but with special attention, often explicit, to the writings of Solinus.

Another thirteenth century map of the same type but now only existing in fragmentary form is the Vercelli map which again has a number of animals depicted on it (Bagrow 1964). There are fewer animals, particularly in the palearctic, which is represented by what might be an aurochs and some sort of large carnivore pursued by a dog. The ethiopian has lions, a camel, a large indeterminate spotted animal, possibly a leopard, a parrot, a falcon and various dragon-lizard animals. In the oriental region there is a domestic elephant, a one horned animal not wholly unlike the Hereford rhinoceros, a spotted yale with tusks, bicorned and cloven hoofed, with some resemblance to the white oriental yale of the Ebstorf map and a bulky bison-like animal together with parrot, falcon and several flying lizards and snakes. Apart from the elephant and the camel, these animals are very considerably more formalised and more difficult to identify than those of the Ebstorf and Hereford maps. The camel has appeared for the first time in the ethiopian region and for the first time as the one humped variety.

Camels are typically palearctic animals, spread to other parts of the world by man. There are two species today, the two humped Bactrian camel from the Gobi-Altai district of the USSR and the one humped camel of Arabia and the northern part of Africa. It is doubtful whether one humped camels are any longer wild but, as domestic animals, they have been spread throughout Africa, India and even to Australia. Because the one humped variety was early spread by man as a beast of burden, it has the appearance of being typical in those various lands where it has been known since comparatively early historic times. Thus camels occur with great frequency and regularity on the maps. One humped domestic camels had been introduced into the north Syrian desert during the seventh century BC at the latest and appear as animals of war on an Assyrian seal of about 648 BC (Smith 1928). Certainly by the first century BC they were known as far south and west as Tunisia. Aristotle distinguished between the two varieties. 'Camels have an exceptional organ wherein they differ from all other animals, and that is the so-called "hump" on their back. The Bactrian camel differs from the Arabian, for the former has two humps and the latter only one' (Thompson 1910).

It is interesting to find that the two humped camels appearing on these early maps are confined to the palearctic region. The Ebstorf map has an excellently woolly two humped camel, with exaggerated cloven hoofs, situated in Palestine (fig 9.1). This might well represent a wild camel. On the Hereford map is a less woolly but still unmistakable two humped camel in the land of Bactria. There seems no doubt that this is the authentic wild Bactrian camel from middle Asia (fig 2.4). The Matthew Paris map of the Holy Land in the thirteenth century (fig 2.5) had a domesticated two humped variety (Bagrow 1964). The only other thirteenth century camel, from the Vercelli map, is the one humped variety, in Africa, well shaped and with

Fig 2.5 Domesticated two humped camel on Matthew Paris's thirteenth century map of the Holy Land in the British Museum, London

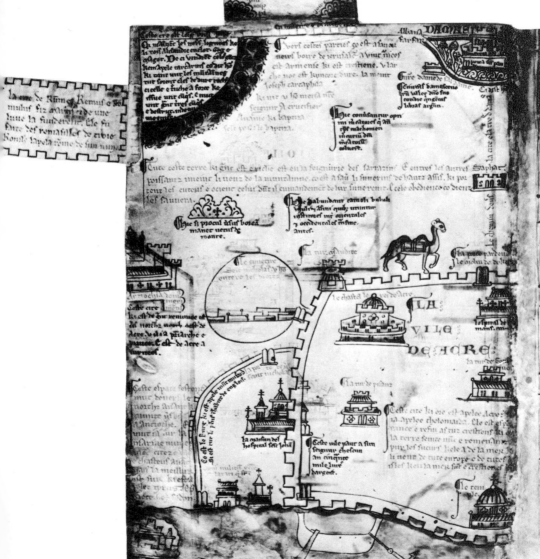

Fig 2.6 One humped camel in Ethiopia on the thirteenth century Vercelli map of the world in the Duomo Vercelli

distinctly cloven hoofs (fig 2.6).

On these early maps, then, lions have been found roaming widespread over the Old World. The palearctic region has already become typified by some cloven hoofed ungulate, a wild ox, a bison or an elk. The ethiopian and oriental regions are correctly depicted with elephants, many birds and reptiles and they are distinguished from one another by the occurrence of the yale only in the oriental region.

Birds and reptiles are, sensibly, particularly abundant in the oriental region. Many, like the basilisks and the dracones in their pictorial representation are difficult to identify with any living animal but are probably to be taken as imaginative pictures based on real but incorrectly observed lizards and snakes. Quick moving reptiles leave only an impression of their shape and colour. According to Pliny, the basilisk 'is a native of the province of Cyrenaica, not more than twelve inches long, and adorned with a bright white marking on the head like a sort of diadem. It routs all snakes with its hiss, and does not move its body forward in manifold coils like the other snakes but advancing with its middle raised high. It kills bushes not only by its touch but also by its breath . . .' (Rackham 1940). This description has usually been taken to refer to the spitting cobra *Naja* but one of the sidewinding vipers, *Cerastes* perhaps, would be described as moving differently from other snakes even though it neither spits nor kills bushes by its breath. Perhaps this basilisk is a mixture of cobra and viper.

Other basilisks have feathered bodies and snakes' tails and may well represent a bird of prey, the drawing compounded from a bird with a snake in its talons. In fact, a Bodleian twelfth century bestiary (MS 764) announces that basilisks eat snakes and figures the crowned bird which, with variations on the tail, resembles the Ebstorf basilisk and recurs on maps for many centuries. Almost certainly basilisks had come to represent the blackish crowned eagles *Circaëtus* of Eurasia and Africa which live almost exclusively on snakes.

More obvious crocodiles, lizards and snakes also abound in the oriental region on these early maps as well as the flying lizard *Draco*, see p. 38.

FOURTEENTH CENTURY MAPS

By the fourteenth century, practical sailing charts had come into use, in conjunction with the magnetic compass, to replace the written periplus of earlier centuries. Catalan and Italian cartographers were foremost in this field and many of these portolans, particularly the Catalan, were in widespread use. The Catalans, based on Majorca and influenced both by the Arabs and by the usual early literature and by their adventurous contemporaries, produced portolans of wider scope than their Italian counterparts. Italian portolans tend to be restricted to the coastlines of the Mediterranean in contrast to the Catalan portolans which are on the scale of world maps, reaching from Scandinavia to China and including a considerable part of north Africa. These Catalan maps are the main source of zoogeographical information in the fourteenth century and, compared with the Ebstorf and Hereford maps, the information is sparse and they add very little to the cumulative knowledge of animal distribution. Yet, at least some of these mapmakers would have had the benefit of the reports brought home by Marco Polo. He described many animals that he encountered on his travels, even giving an accurate account of a rhinoceros but calling it a unicorn. His rhinoceros is depicted, a bit

Fig 2.7 Three toed ostrich, domestic camel, domestic elephant and a bird of prey in north Africa; falcon in Norway on Dulcert's portolan of 1339 in the Bibliothèque Nationale, Paris

far north but marginally in the oriental region, on the map painted on the wall of the Doge's Palace in Venice.

When animals appear on the fourteenth century portolans, Africa is linked with the camel and the elephant. An ostrich occurs in Africa on the Catalan portolan of Angelo Dulcert in 1339 (Nordenskiöld 1897) and a parrot on the Venetian chart of the Pizigano brothers in 1367 (Jomard 1854). This is not the first occurrence of ostriches for they were represented on the Ebstorf and Hereford maps also though, in spite of its incorrectly drawn three toes, the Dulcert ostrich is a superior representation to either of the two earlier ones (fig 2.7). The Hereford ostrich, however, was correctly two toed, though somewhat northerly in distribution. Falcons make their appearance as representative animals of the palearctic and, on all these maps, only the elephant has wandered too far north, on the Paris Catalan map of Abraham Cresques (Bagrow 1964) and the Venice map of Marco Polo's travels but, since these elephants were domesticated, saddled and driven, their position is understandable.

The Gough map of Great Britain in the Bodleian Library (about 1360) merits notice for the occurrence on it of a wolf in the county of Sutherland with the remark 'hic ha bundant lupi' and, near Loch Ness, a deer 'hic maxima venaccio'.

Although the fourteenth century maps cannot be considered remarkable for increasing knowledge of the fauna of the known world, they are interesting in two other ways. Firstly, while the boundaries of the world were not increasing in any spectacular way on the maps, knowledge of peculiar animals was coming in from many sources, in particular from the accounts of the travels of Marco Polo, so that it was by now far too ambitious a project to attempt to put all the animals of a continent into the space on a map. There may have been vast empty spaces but it is unlikely they would hold all the animals known to exist in them. After the exuberance of the animals on some thirteenth century maps there was already, then, a tendency to restrict the numbers of animals on the maps to a few that were considered typical of the continent: the camel, the elephant and the ostrich, for instance, were becoming symbols of Africa and the falcon a symbol of the European parts of the palearctic.

Secondly, there had been a noticeable improvement in the accuracy of representation of some of the animals, an accuracy greater than many contemporary bestiary illustrations. The Catalan one humped camel of Abraham Cresques and those of Dulcert are cloven hoofed with an indication of the pad-like quality of the feet and given an excellent impressionist rendering of a camel (fig 2.7). All these camels are domestic animals, either shown in company of men or shown saddled and bridled. The elephants, too, are more carefully drawn than those of the previous century, though they still show considerable variation in the number of toes and the position of their ears. Dulcert's African elephant has large feet with four toes, large ears and long tusks. The tusks of the elephants curl upwards, extravagantly, but the general impression is that they are curling in this unlikely manner correctly from the upper jaw (fig 2.7). There was a good deal of disagreement over the provenance of these valuable teeth possibly because of the somewhat ambiguous guidance given by Oppian about AD 212. 'For such growths from the upper jaws of wild beasts as are horny, spring upward: if they incline downward they are certainly teeth . . . Of these two horns of the Elephant the roots first of all spring from the head, mighty as the head is mighty, even as the roots of the oak; then below, concealed by the skin where they meet the temples, they project into the jaw; and when left bare by the jaws they give to the vulgar the false impression of teeth' (Mair 1958).

As late as 1491, an elephant is drawn in a book of natural history *Ortus Sanitatis* by J. von Cube with the tusks representing lower jaw teeth and Cadomosto reported that 'these elephants have two large teeth at each side of their mouths that is, one on each side like the wild boar, but set in the lower jaw. There is no difference save that the points of the teeth of the boar are turned upwards, while those of the elephant are turned downwards towards the ground' (Crone 1937). However, other explorers described the opposite: 'the two great teeth or tuskes, are placed in the highest jawe' (Lewes Vertomanus 1503, Eden 1555). But this interesting fact had to be rediscovered by John Lok in 1555 (Hakluyt 1598) and was forgotten again twenty years later in Münster and Belle Forest's *La cosmographie universelle de tout le monde*. One way and another, there was considerable doubt and controversy over this simple anatomical fact. Interesting, in so far as the elephant had been a well known domestic and show animal, particularly during the Roman Empire. It is represented accurately on many Roman decorative objects, such as medals and in statuary. But it lost its domestic use in Europe during the Middle

Ages, and there were few specimens to be seen from then until the sixteenth century. Its anatomy had to be continually rediscovered and yet it lived on through the maps and bestiaries of the Middle Ages as an animal representative of either Africa or India or both.

FIFTEENTH CENTURY MAPS

The main advances in the knowledge of the world during the fifteenth century as depicted in the maps of the period was an increase in accuracy of the lands bordering the Mediterranean and an extension

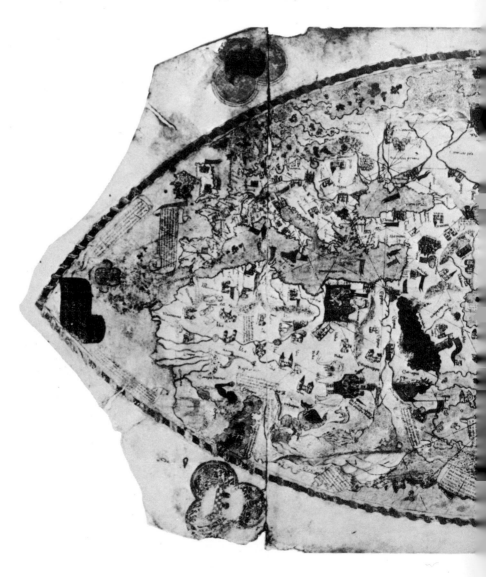

of the coasts of Africa and the East Indies. Voyages southwards along the coasts of Africa were gradually increasing in length and, by the middle of the century, the more southerly part of Africa was known not to turn eastwards but to continue south, although the Cape was not rounded until 1487 and a fairly modern representation

Fig 2.8 The Genoese world map of 1457 in the Biblioteca Nazionale, Florence: elephant, camel, lion, monkeys, giraffe, dragon and crocodile in the ethiopian region; griffon or black vulture, leopard, ox and polar bear in the palearctic region; snake and storks in the oriental region

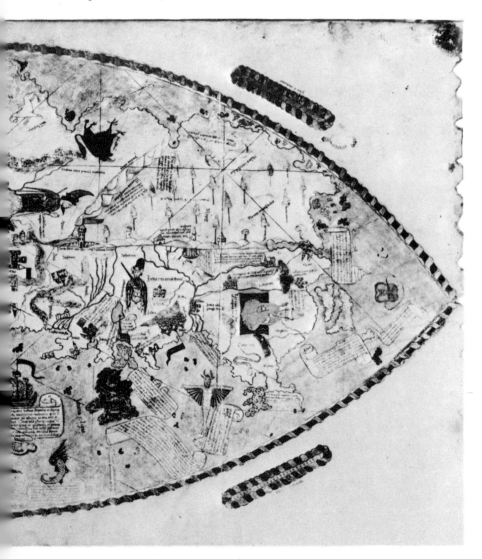

of Africa does not appear on maps until towards the end of the century (Henricus Martellus about 1490 in Bagrow 1964, for example). Advances towards the spice islands of the East Indies and southern China had also been made by the middle of the century. The Venetian, Nicolo de Conti, in 1444, had reported the existence of Ceylon and Sumatra again (Penzer 1937) and these islands were drawn into the mid-century map of Fra Mauro (Bagrow 1964). The accuracy of the coastline of India itself was improving and, to the east, there had been an extension to islands which may represent the Moluccas.

The introduction of Ptolemy's *Geographia* to western Europe in manuscript form in 1406, the technological improvement in navigation instruments and improvements in the ships themselves all contributed to the profound advances in geographical knowledge during the fifteenth century. By the end of the century, the development of printing presses extended the availability of maps. The *Geographia* was printed, with maps, in 1477. From the end of the century dates the earliest known globe to have survived, that of Martin Behaim made in 1492 (Ravenstein 1908).

The extension of knowledge of the coastline of Africa was not paralleled by any marked increase in zoological knowledge. On world maps of the century the ethiopian region is still mainly symbolised by the camels and elephants of the previous century although they were by now becoming less exclusively domesticated representatives of their species and being more accurately drawn. The most striking advance, however, was the depiction of a recognisable giraffe (fig 2.8) on the Genoese world map of 1457 (Bagrow 1964).

This was the first time an accurate giraffe had represented Africa although camelopardalis had appeared much earlier in the ethiopian region of the Ebstorf map (fig 2.2). Camelopardalis, however, was only a giraffe by name, being a four clawed spotted animal with a normally short neck.

But although a map had to wait for a well proportioned giraffe until 1457, giraffes had been known accurately and depicted accurately as representatives of the land of the Nile at least as far back as the third century BC. Beautiful illustrations of these and many other African animals, lions, onagra, monkeys, a rhinoceros and a hippo are depicted on the Barberini mosaic *L'Inondazione del Nilo* preserved in Italy at Palestrina (fig 2.9). These animals were more accurate than any that occurred on maps before the sixteenth and seventeenth centuries. Strabo had described the camelopards: ' . . . though they are in no respect like leopards, for the dappled marking of their skin is more like that of a fawnskin, which latter is flecked with spots, and their hinder parts are so much lower than their front parts that they appear to be seated on their tail-parts, which have the height of an ox, although their forelegs are no shorter than those of camels . . .' To which Pliny could add 'feet and legs like an ox, and a head like a camel'. And many years later, in about 1362, Mandeville commented: 'and he may well enough stand on the earth and look over a high house' (Letts 1953).

The ethiopian region continues to be represented by large carnivores: lions range through the Africa of several of the later world maps and, on the Behaim globe of 1492, a mongoose is shown in west Africa attacking a snake. Crocodiles and monkeys inhabit Ethiopia and, on a fifteenth century portolan fragment in the Biblioteca Estense in Modena occurs, in company with a crocodile and a lion, a cumbersome animal in shape like the later portrayal of rhinoceroses but with nothing more than two lumps on the head (fig 2.10). This rhinoceros is very different from the slender animal of the Hereford map and the bestiaries but bears some resemblance

Fig. 2.9 Part of the mosaic *L'Inondazione del Nilo*, third century BC, Palestrina

D

to the much earlier rhinos of the Italian mosaics. Like its predecessors it has claws on its heavy feet.

Of the birds, the ostrich seems to have been growing in importance as an African type, becoming two toed once more and becoming more splendidly aggressive and ostrich-like in, for instance, he 1497 *Carta Nautica* of Jehuda ben Zara (fig 2.11). Snakes and dragons are frequent at this time.

In the palearctic the animal assemblage is different. It continues the tradition of the earlier maps and adds to it. Boar, wolf and lion inhabit the far north of Mecia de Viladestes' Catalan chart of about 1413 (Marcel 1896). Foxes and bears occur in the 1492 Behaim globe palearctic and, in 1457 on the Genoese world map, there is a white carnivore in the northern regions which could represent, though not with noticeable accuracy, either an arctic fox or a polar bear. At about the same time, the decorative Borgia map of the world, engraved on

Fig 2.10 Lion, crocodile and probably a rhinoceros in Africa on an anonymous fifteenth century portolan fragment in the Biblioteca Estense, Modena

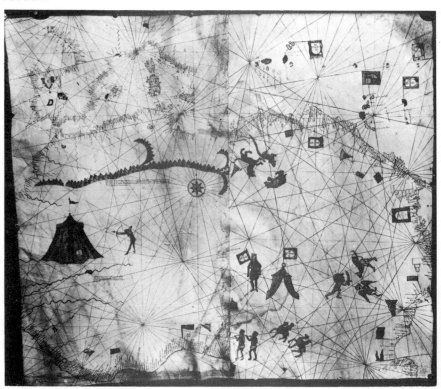

metal some time between 1410 and 1458, portrays a definite polar bear emerging from an igloo in Norway.

Falcons continue to represent the palearctic and, in particular, the northern ungulates continue often in association with falconry. A deer occurs in Norway and a domesticated reindeer or stag takes part in falconry further east in 1413. A reindeer again helps to represent the palearctic region on the Florence Catalan map of 1439 (Cortesão 1954). An elk and similarly domesticated reindeer occur on the Borgia map, oxen draw a cart on the Genoese map, horses and a reindeer are domesticated on the Modena Catalan world map of 1450 (Bagrow 1964).

Africa and the palearctic are given the most animals. The expanding areas of the east are left mainly empty, in contrast to the earlier efforts to colonise it with birds, serpents, unicorns, dragons, elephants and cloven hoofed ungulates. Only two maps of the fifteenth century contribute animals to the oriental region, the Genoese world map which permits a snake to inhabit the area and the Borgia map which, in its formalised exuberance resembling the twelfth century maps, populates the oriental region with camels, jackals or hyenas, an elephant, a panther, lion, dragon and, marginally in the region, some reptile.

Again the most striking feature of these maps is the rarity with which errors in placing of the animals occurs. But it should also be recognised that, apart from remarkably improved accuracy of drawing by the end of the century (particularly the Jehuda ben Zara and Ancona portolans, de Santarem 1849), the Hereford and Ebstorf maps are much fuller as essays in zoogeographical mapmaking. Camelopardalis of the Ebstorf map may have looked less like a giraffe than that of the Genoese world map but it did record one of the most typical animals of the ethiopian region by name and an animal which, like the ostrich, is confined to the region. Already, by the sixth century, Cosmos was aware that giraffes were typically ethiopian animals and could report that 'the cameleopard is found only in Ethiopia. These also are wild beasts and have not been domesticated. But in the palace (at Axum in Abyssinia) they have one or two which they have tamed by the king's command by catching them when young, in order to keep them for show' (Yule and Cordier 1915).

Other typical ethiopian animals such as hippos had been described from the Nile by Herodotus: 'the animal has four legs, cloven hoofs like an ox, a snub nose, a horse's mane and tail, conspicuous tusks, a voice like a horse's neigh, and is about the size of a very large ox. Its hide is so thick and tough that when dried it can be made into spear-shafts'. Hippos had symbolised the, Nile in the Barberini mosaics and those of Pompeii but they do not appear on maps of Africa until 1542.

In contrast, anteating mammals occur in Africa on the early maps although whether they represent the most obvious endemic African anteater, the aardvark, or one of the other animals that feeds on ants' and termites' nests is open to dispute. Aardvarks had been well

Fig 2.11 Ostrich, camel and elephant in Africa on the nautical chart of Jehuda ben Zara 1497 in the Biblioteca Vaticana

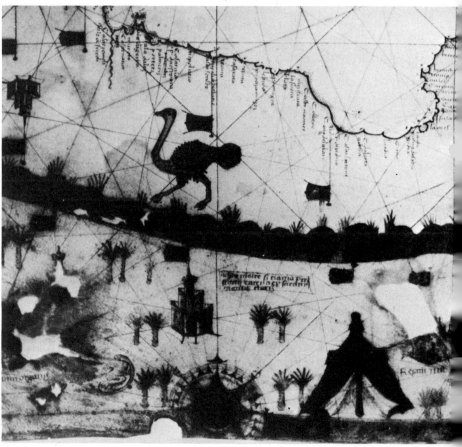

enough known in prehistoric times to figure on the walls of Tassili rock shelters.

Mirmicaleon occurs in Ethiopia on the Ebstorf map (fig 2.2) and there, too, the Hereford map reports: 'hinc grandes formice auream sericam arenas'. Other than that they seem to be ant or termite eating animals, that dig into the nests or into sand for their prey, it is difficult to decide on a particular animal to equate with either the name or the indeterminate drawing of the Ebstorf map. There are a number of anteaters in Africa and several also in the oriental region but not all are shared by the two regions. The observations of the early writers

Fig 2.12 Borgia map of the world engraved on iron between 1410 and 1458 in the Biblioteca Vaticana: deer and polar bear in the palearctic region (at the bottom); elephant in the oriental region (on the left)

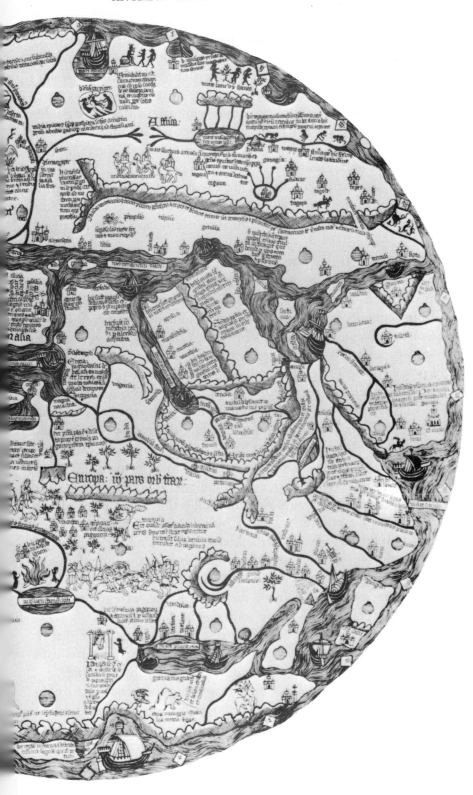

that mirmicaleon occurred in other parts of the world beside Africa narrows the choice a little. Agartharchides, about 182 BC, reported that mirmicaleon inhabited Arabia (Müller 1855) and Strabo describes them from both Africa and India, golden in colour and less hairy in Africa than in India. Pangolins, the scaly anteaters *Manis*, are golden but, although some species of Indian pangolin have more hair than others, it would be difficult to describe the fircone-like pangolin as hairy. Ratels or honey badgers also occur in both regions. Whichever anteater is chosen it must be admitted to be a guess. But it is interesting to have an anteating animal designated in the ethiopian region. More obvious representations of other anteaters occur later on in the maps, see pp. 75, 131 and 164.

The little known African insectivore and rodent families that are confined to the region are not superficially different enough from the European forms to merit representation on maps. Herodotus described rodents of three families from the nomads country of Libya: 'There are, however, three kinds of mice, called respectively *dipodes* [jerboas of the family Dipodidae with long tails and long hind legs well known to the Egyptians and included on many of their murals and modelled faience in the twelfth century (Brion 1959) and characteristic of Old World deserts], *zegeries* [possibly the gerbils or sand rats a subfamily of the Cricetidae found in the drier parts of the Old World] and *echines* [probably the spiny mice *Acomys* a near-desert version of the more usual house and field mice Muridae].' These strikingly different types of mice do not appear on maps. The largest and most spectacular animals were naturally those that were picked out to represent a continent, being more obviously different from the animals at home than smaller animals like mice might seem to be.

Thus, at the end of the fifteenth century, before the boundaries of the world were to be pushed out in a spectacular way, the zoogeography of the world, read from the maps alone, extends to three regions: the ethiopian, palearctic and oriental.

The ethiopian region is mainly represented by camels, elephants, ostriches, lions, antelopes, smaller carnivores, parrots, basilisks (crowned eagles), snakes, lizards and, occasionally, by a giraffe.

The palearctic is depicted as the home of deer, wild oxen or aurochs and other ungulates of various sorts, camels, bears (sometimes white), lions, eagles and falcons.

The oriental contains serpents, dragons and birds, with the occasional elephant and ungulate.

There is little to quarrel with in this pictorial representation of the regions. Deer are abundant in Europe and Asia. Bears, while occurring in the palearctic, are, like deer, absent from Africa. Elephants, a multitude of reptiles and pheasant-like birds, give a tolerably good impression of the oriental region (George 1962).

III

Neotropical Region

Towards the end of the fifteenth century the great Portuguese voyages of discovery were pushing out the limits of the known world. In 1487, Diaz had sailed round the Cape and, in 1492, Columbus sailed from Europe to the spice islands and found instead the New World. Both these achievements were further consolidated in the years immediately following their discoveries. Vasco da Gama, Amerigo Vespucci and Cabral had all visited South America by the turn of the century and, in 1497, John Cabot had sailed towards Cathay in the north and discovered Newfoundland.

Cartographers were not slow to record these discoveries and, during the first twenty years or so of the century, numerous new maps of the world appeared, including for the first time, unless the recent dating of about 1440 for the Yale map is accepted (Skelton, Marston & Painter 1965), the continent of America, specifying the shape of Africa, Madagascar and extending the boundaries of south east Asia and of China and Japan (Levillier 1948).

THE DISCOVERY OF THE FAUNA OF SOUTH AMERICA

Many maps drawn at this time had pictures of animals on them although for the most part the animals were concentrated in one or two regions only. During the century, only two maps of the world had animals depicted over three or more regions and could thus be considered as contributing to a general knowledge of animal distribution.

The new animals of South America had an obvious attraction and the early maps of the century were those depicting the South American fauna for the first time.

The early visitors to the West Indies, Central and South America had all reported the huge and brilliantly coloured parrots of the region, commenting particularly on their length and the diversity of their colouring.

Columbus had reported seeing snakes and rats (probably a hutia of the family Capromyidae) as well as a great number of parrots and, in 1493, reported from Haiti that 'there is further an animal the colour of a rabbit with similar fur, it is the size of a young rabbit, has a long tail, and hind and fore feet like those of a rat. These animals climb trees and many who have eaten them say that the flesh is very good.' This description of a hutia seems to fit the zagouti *Plagiodontia* recently described as of robust form with small ears and a naked tail of moderate length (Ellerman 1940) and as 'slow-moving, inoffensive, feeds on fruit and vegetables, able to climb well . . . and being largely eaten, judging from the quantities of remains found in caves and native kitchen middens . . .' (Burton 1962). On the third voyage, the narrative of Columbus includes monkeys on the mainland, inland from Trinidad and, from his fourth voyage in 1502, he recorded lions (pumas *Profelis*), stags, fallow deer and peccaries (Jane 1930).

Meanwhile, from the mainland further south, Vespucci had written in 1500 of birds, lions, panthers (ocelots or jaguars), catamounts (pumas again), wolves, baboons, hogs, goats, stags, hares, rabbits and, particularly, of parrots: 'some were crimson-coloured, others of variegated green and lemon, others entirely green and others again that were black and flesh-coloured' adding that all the animals were quite different from any he had seen anywhere else (Levillier 1951).

Cabral, too, reported from Brazil parrots of many and different colours and his companions Cretico and Marchioni wrote in 1501 of the large size of these birds: 'They brought back two parrots of different colours which are an arm and a half long' (Greenlee 1938).

It is not surprising that the early cartographers picked on the most spectacular and most often reported animals of the new continent to illuminate their maps which contained the New World for probably the first time. The macaws, an endemic South American group of the parrot family, occurring in many colours from mainly scarlet or mixed bright colours to blue and mainly green, are the members of that fauna which first come to represent the continent on maps and

Fig 3.1 World chart of Nicolo de Caveri 1502 in the Bibliothèque
Nationale, Paris

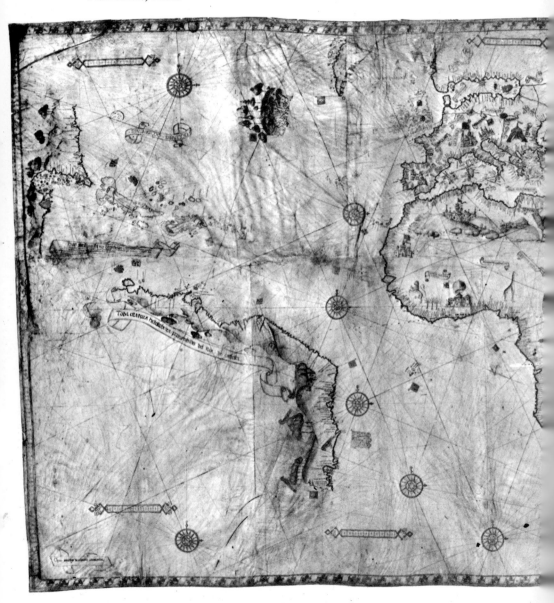

which persisted through three centuries as symbolic of the neotropical region. Thus, in 1502, a Portuguese MS map of the world called the Cantino planisphere, based on the discoveries of Vasco da Gama, Vespucci, Cabral and Corte Real, shows the macaws *Ara* of South America for the first time (Bagrow 1964). They have long tails and are gorgeously coloured in red, blue and yellow and contrast with the correctly much smaller and more sober green Senegal parrot *Poicephalus senegalus* and grey, red tailed parrots *Psittacus erithacus* of the ethiopian region. In the same year, 1502, Nicolo de Caveri of Genoa also drew long tailed parrots, or macaws, sitting in the trees on the east coast of the neotropical region, this time they were uniformly red (fig 3.1). And, in 1507, Waldseemüller, basing his map on the exploits of the Portuguese and the Caveri map, whose influence on cartography was to persist until Mercator's time, had one parrot *ruber psitans* in South America (Bagrow 1964). Waldseemüller's map was a woodcut and one of the first printed maps of the world. With the advent of woodcuts and copper engravings, maps began to have a wider circulation.

No extensions to the general picture took place until 1513 when a map made by the Turkish hydrographer Piri Re'is, based on a map of Columbus, showed a large number of mammals for the first time, in South America, together with some snakes and the symbolic parrots, green now with red beaks and long tails, sitting on all the Caribbean islands (Yusuf Akçura 1935), but described as being of four kinds: white, red, green and black (fig 3.2). There were monkeys with long tails, a one horned bovid, a two horned spotted ungulate with a tusk, remarkably like the yale of the Vercelli map, a six horned animal, which might possibly be one of the South American hollow toothed deer with much branched antlers, and an animal that might well represent a llama were it not for the horns. Piri Re'is seems to have imagined all South American ungulates with the most spectacular twisted or branched horns. Apart from these adornments, the animals bear considerable likenesses to some of the neotropical ungulates. This is further supported by some of the inscriptions on the map. For instance, 'in this territory there are white-haired creatures shaped like this and six horned cows are also found' (Kahle 1956) would seem nearly to confirm the interpretation of llama and South American deer. A single carnivore, looking agile with its tail flourishing, resembles the very common South American martens or tayras

Fig 3.2 Drawings from the Piri Re'is map of 1513 based on a map of Columbus: macaw, yale, six horned cow and horned llama

(mustelids) but could, perhaps, represent the larger, more frightening and, therefore, more written about jaguar.

Three years later, a mammal arrived on a map which was to become almost as frequent as the parrot as a representative of the neotropical region. This was an opossum (fig 3.3) drawn on the 1516 Waldseemüller woodcut *Carta Marina* (Bagrow 1964). Described on the map as having a pouch under its belly where it puts its young except when they were let out to suckle, it was more fully described by Vincent Agnes Pinzon in 1499: 'Between these Trees he saw as strange a Monster, the foremost part resembling a Fox, the hinder a Monkey, the feet were like a mans, with ears like an owl; under whose Belly hung a great Bag, in which it carry'd the young, which they drop not, nor forsake till they can feed themselves.' Pinzon caught one of them with three young, which died on the voyage, but the dam he presented alive in Granada to the King (Ogilby 1671). Pietro Martieri in *Four Decades*, written about 1520, wrote: 'among the trees is found that monstrous beaste with a snout like a foxe, a tayle like a marmosette, eares lyke a bat, handes lyke a man, and feete lyke an ape, bearying her whelpes aboute with her in an outwarde bellye much lyke unto a great bagge or purse' (Eden 1555). In each of its separate features Waldseemüller's opossum bears a striking resemblance to the real animal although, when put together, the total somehow looks less like an opossum than it might. Its fox-like head, the animal received the name of simivulpe eventually, primate-like hands and feet, together with the pouch, are diagnostic of the American opossums. In other features, the length of the tail and the colour and length of the coat, the animals show considerable variation through their long range from North America to the southern parts of South America. Waldseemüller's opossum had shaggy hair and a short tail, in contrast to Pietro Martieri's with a marmoset tail, and is typical of the north and mountain areas. This particular animal of Waldseemüller was traced off on to many later maps, sometimes facing one way, sometimes the other and becoming progressively more formalised.

So, at this stage, long tailed parrots, long tailed monkeys and an animal with a pouch were considered representative of South America.

THE FAUNA INCREASES

Then, in 1527, the South American ostrich or rhea turns up for the first time, on the Spanish Wolfenbüttel map of the New World, attributed to the Portuguese cartographer Ribeiro (Cortesão & Teixeira da Mota 1960). Antonio Pigafetta, whose influence on the mapmaking of Ribeiro is well known, had listed several birds from South America, among which was an ostrich (Robertson 1906).

Two years later, Ribeiro redrew a map of the world and covered it with animals (Almagià 1948). To the monkeys, opossums, rheas and parrots that were becoming familiars of the South American scene, he added deer, a jaguar, a possible bear, a dragon, some birds and a number of small animals that are difficult to interpret but, on the original preserved in the Vatican library, they give an impression of some of the South American rodents such as the mara, chinchilla and viscacha. If this interpretation is correct, this is the first occurrence on a map of a representative of the New World rodents. These conspicuous continental forms were not described in writing until 1589. 'Chinchillas are another genus of small animals like squirrels having a marvellously soft fur, and its skin is taken for giving as a present and as a wholesome cover for the stomach and for parts where it is necessary to keep a moderate heat; also they make coverings, or blankets of the fur of the chinchillas. They are found in the sierra of Peru where there are also other commoner animals, which are called guinea pigs, which the Indians consider very good as food, and often use these guinea pigs as offering in their sacrifices. They are like rabbits and have their burrows under the earth, and in some parts they undermine the whole place. Some are brown, others white and different. Other animals are called vizcachas, which are a sort of hare, some bigger, and also hunted' (Acosta 1608).

Among the animals on Ribeiro's map there occurs an animal with every appearance of an armadillo: its small pig-like body with an impression of armouring seems to identify it (fig 10.1).

Fig 3.3 The first opossum in South America on Waldseemüller's woodcut *Carta Marina* of 1516 in Schloss Wolfegg

Faintly, there appears an animal which, in view of later pictures, probably represents a howler monkey.

Alonso de Santa Cruz in 1540 (Wieser 1908) depicted llamas for the first time, with the possible exception of Re'is in 1513. In 1520, Pigafetta, recording Magellan's voyage through the Straits of Magellan, had already described one of the llamas: 'its head and ears of the size of a mule, and the neck and body of the fashion of a camel, the legs of a deer and the tail like that of a horse' (Stanley 1874). The llamas on Alonso de Santa Cruz map (fig 3.4) resemble closely Pigafetta's description. In spite of these 1540 map llamas, a recent author (Delaunay 1962) claims that the first European drawing of a llama occurred at Antwerp in 1558, when a live animal arrived there from Peru.

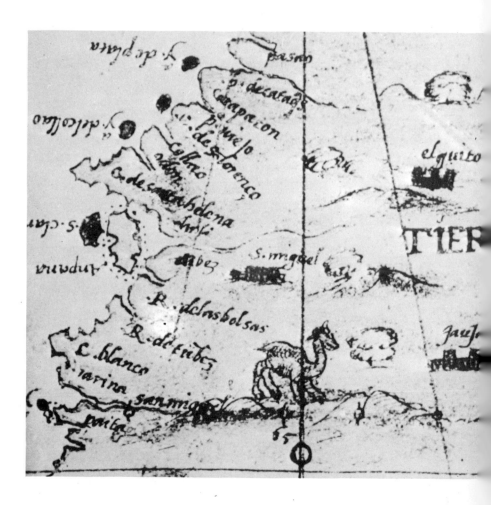

Llamas belong to the same family as the camels, sharing many of their well known characteristics: amenable to domestication, though unfriendly, providing not only admirable pack animals capable of long distances over bad surfaces but also providing wool suitable for cloth making and flesh for eating. Perhaps it was these last features that led many of the early writers to describe them as large sheep, recognising among them at least three varieties, the woolly pacos (alpaca), vicunas (with silky hair) and the guanacos or llamas, the all purpose domesticated variety. The long tailed woolly sheep that appear on the maps are, in all probability, representational of the pacos; the more camel-like pack animals are guanacos or llamas.

By 1551 this distinction had appeared in the South America of the world map of Sancho Gutiérrez, in the Österreichische National-

Fig 3.4 Llamas on part of a map of America 1540 by Alonso de Santa Cruz in *Islario General*

bibliothek in Vienna (and see Wagner 1951). There are the woolly sheep-like pacos, the camel-like guanacos and, possibly, the more slender vicunas, described by Acosta in 1589: 'These vicunas are greater than goates, and lesse than calves. Their haire is of the colour of dried roses, somewhat clearer, they have no hornes like stagges and goates. They feede upon the highest tops of the mountains . . . There are two kindes of these sheepe or llamas, the one they call Pacos, or sheepe bearing wooll, and the others bare, and have little wooll, so are they better for burthen: they are bigger than great sheepe, and lesse than calves, they have a very long necke, like to a camel, whereof they have good neede, for, being high of stature, they have need of a long necke, else should they be deformed. They are of diverse colours, some all white, others all blacke, some grey and some spotted'. On the maps of South America, llamas and their relatives had come to stay.

In 1541 a terrestrial globe of Mercator showed not only an opossum but also a manatee and a recognisable aquatic iguanid lizard.

Iguanas, which had been reported by Columbus in 1492–1493 and correctly described as having spiked ridges down their backs by Enciso in 1518, 'also there is another sort of them called yaguanas and be as big as the lagartus, and thei have a round hedde and from the forehed to the tail upon his backe ther goeth a rydge of sharpe prickes standing up very grislie. Their be of fier colour and some what specled, and these go in the montaynes and be very fearfull to loke on but thei be not noyfull . . .' (Taylor 1931), are typical lizards of the New World, reaching sometimes very large sizes on some of the islands.

Monkeys and rheas, parrots and opossums persisted until, in 1546, another typical South American creature appeared, with certainty this time, on a world map of the Dieppe school of cartographers (fig 3.5) by Desceliers (Jomard 1854). This was the peccary, which had been recorded by Columbus 1502 from Panama and by Vespucci 1500 from South America but which had not been depicted before

Fig 3.5 The neotropical fauna from Desceliers' map of the world 1546 in the John Rylands Library, Manchester: domestic llamas, opossum, peccary and alligator in the north; snakes, monkey, dragon, large rodent, armadillo and four legged rheas in the south; long tailed turtle in the east

unless the grey, tusked but horned, animal of Piri Re'is 1513 is permitted. The Dieppe school, of which the most famous cartographers are Desceliers, Vallard and Le Testu, is known to have derived its cartographic information from Portuguese sources and it is interesting to find on these maps animals, too, that had been reported from Portuguese sources such as Columbus.

An armadillo is distinctly recognisable by this time. There is a long tailed turtle, a lizard with wings and some sort of other reptile, possibly an alligator or caiman, to represent the other vertebrates. Llamas and monkeys persist and so supposedly does the opossum, although by now it looks more like a pouched cow. Birds that are presumably rheas have four legs. There is also an animal that might conceivably be a capybara, or other large South American rodent, which has turned up already on another Dieppe map, the 1536 Harleian or Dauphin map in the British Museum.

Desceliers' later map of 1550, also in the British Museum, drops all these interesting animals and symbolises South America by monkeys and macaws once again.

The maps of the first half of the sixteenth century show the gradually increasing knowledge of the South American fauna as it was becoming known in Europe through the writings of the early explorers and chroniclers. From the early macaws, progress had been rapid.

First came the monkeys, with large eyes and long tails, members of the cebid, flat nosed group. Together with the marmoset family, the cebids are confined to the neotropical region, forming a typical element in its fauna. They are only distantly related to the more dog nosed monkeys of the Old World. The monkeys were followed on the maps by the opossum, noted for its pouch and thus belonging to one of the only two families of marsupial mammals known outside Australia. The other neotropical marsupial family, which consists of mouse-like animals, only became known to zoologists in the middle of the nineteenth century.

Of the typical bird families of South America, the rhea arrived in 1527 to be a comparatively frequent member of the map faunas.

Rheas were followed by llamas and the peccary.

Peccaries are related to the Old World pigs but form a distinct family, which is both confined to the New World and is the only type of wild pig found there. It is essentially a northern form that has migrated south into the neotropical region. Peccaries differ from Old World pigs in their tooth pattern, the lesser development of the canines and in the greater fusion of the bones of the hind feet, a feature most astutely, if incorrectly in detail, recognised by Pietro Martieri, in the *Second Decade*, when he wrote: 'They differ also from ours in theyr feete: for theyr hinder feete are whole undivided, and also without any hoofe' (Eden 1555). The more usual descriptions, such as those of Pigafetta 1520 and Acosta 1589, confused the issue by referring to peccaries as 'swine which have their navels on their backs' though this peculiar characteristic was not represented on the peccaries drawn on the maps.

The next typical animal of the neotropical region to be added to the maps had been the armadillo, also in 1527. Armadillos had been described by Enciso in 1518 and, in greater detail, by later chroniclers such as Barlow in 1540. 'Also ther is a kynde of small beastes no bigger than a pigges of a moneth olde, and the fete the hede and the eares be like a horse, and his bodie and his head is all covered saving his eres with a shell moche like the shell of a tortuga, but it is the very proportion of an armed horse for this shelle hangeth downe by his sides and afore his brest moving as it were hanged by gynowes [hinges], or moche like the lappes of a complete harneis. It is an admiration to behold it. Hit fedeth like a horse and his taile is like a pigges taile, saving it is straight' (Taylor 1931).

Armadillos belong to a family of the Edentata, an order of mammals virtually confined to South America, originating there and comprising the anteaters and sloths as well as the armoured armadillos. A few species spread north into the United States of which only the nine banded armadillo remains today.

Less certain is the record of South American rodents, on the maps of Ribeiro and Desceliers. Of the ten families that are confined to South America, it is possible that at least three were intended on the maps: the mara *Dolichotis* (family Caviidae); the viscacha *Lagostomus* or *Lagidium* and the chinchilla (both in the family Chinchillidae), in 1527 for the first time; and the capybara *Hydrochaerus* (family Hydrochaeridae) in 1536. Certainly rodents had been observed and described by the earliest explorers, though it is not always easy to decide which genus or even which family they refer to. Thus, the references to rabbits or hares, 'conies like unto hares, both in colour and bignesse', according to Pietro Martieri in about 1526 (Eden 1555), might have applied to the viscachas or other members of the chinchilla family and the references just to animals like conies probably applied to the agoutis or pacas similar to, but larger than, the well known hutias from the islands, 'animals called conies and utias which are small conies' reported by the Venetian Porcacchi in 1572.

The hutias (Capromyidae) had been described from the first expeditions to the West Indian islands and several genera were known. Alonso de Santa Cruz described, in 1540, short tailed hutias *Geocapromys* 'without tails and ears like a mouse' and zagoutis *Plagiodontia* 'with tails like mice' but, as far as can be seen, they are not obviously represented on the maps.

The deer (hollow toothed deer Odocoileinae), tigers (the usual name for jaguars) and lions (pumas) that occur from time to time on the maps are animals that, though not so distinctive, do in fact occur typically in South America. The depiction of them on the maps was probably as much to show that there were some familiar animals in the New World as to record their distinctiveness. However, many writers, among them Vespucci in 1504, observed that these animals differed from those that lived in the Old World in that '. . . few are like ours, except the lions, panthers, stags, boars, goats and deer; and even these have some dissimilarities of form . . .' (Levillier 1951).

Apart from the thirteen diverse families of neotropical rodents, ten of which are confined to the region and which may or may not have already been given representation, there are five other families of mammals that are confined to this neotropical region, which extends from the coastal regions of Mexico to Cape Horn and includes the Caribbean islands. These five indigenous mammal families are the caenolestids a family of mouse-like marsupials, the marmosets, the cebid monkeys, the sloths and the anteaters. Of these, only the cebid monkeys had so far appeared on the maps.

South America shares with North America and only with North America four mammalian families: opossums, armadillos, arboreal porcupines and peccaries, all but the last of which are primarily neotropical. All these families had been represented as symbolic of the continent. None of these families is found depicted in any other part of the world on world maps and, therefore, they cannot be the result of fortuitous scattering of animals, an irresponsible filling of empty spaces, nor can they be interpreted as, naïvely, a simple desire to picture newly discovered animals.

Furthermore, the llamas, related only to the palearctic camels, the deer, jaguars and pumas are all features of the fauna, though distinct from their relatives in other parts of the world only at generic level.

Even the apparent exceptions, the quaint horned beasts of Piri Re'is and the winged reptiles of Desceliers, may have been drawings of what those authors believed they had understood from the early writing available but, whatever the explanation, the unreal depiction was not repeated and it must, therefore, be recognised that serious attempts at accuracy were being made to compile an overall picture of the South American fauna.

As the knowledge of the continent widened so the faunistic elements increased. In fact, by 1550 a very fair representation of the South American fauna could be obtained from maps though, of course, no one map contained all the animals. Thus, in addition to the mammals, the macaws (confined genera), the rhea (a confined family), a motley collection of unidentified birds (to signify, perhaps, the Bird Continent as South America has been called) together with a few snakes and the iguanid lizards, alligators or caimans (occurring first, in 1547, on the South America of the Vallard atlas, now in the Huntington Library of San Marino California, to occur frequently afterwards) completed the vertebrate fauna of South America to the mid-sixteenth century.

GREAT ANTEATERS, HOWLERS AND TOUCANS

The second half of the sixteenth century opens with the 1551 world map of Sancho Gutiérrez, whose range of llamas has already been described. In addition, his rivers contain alligators or caimans, there is a monkey, a parrot and many other birds. But more exuberant is the work of Guillaume Le Testu. His *Cosmographie Universelle* 1555 and world map of 1566, both in the Bibliothèque Nationale in Paris, abound in interesting animals, some of which are reminiscent of Piri Re'is, others more easily identified.

In the 1555 manuscript atlas, South America seems to increase its population of rodents, though it is not certain that these do not represent some of the smaller carnivores of the region. However, a large eared animal gives an overall impression of being hare-like, an impression supported by its likeness to some of the early drawings of lagomorphs (Megenberg 1481, for example) and can, perhaps, be

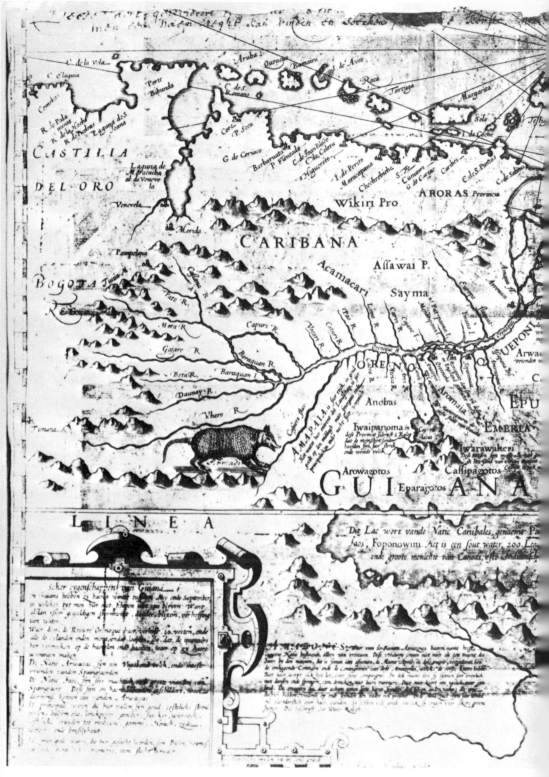

Fig 3.6 Map of Guiana by Hondius 1599

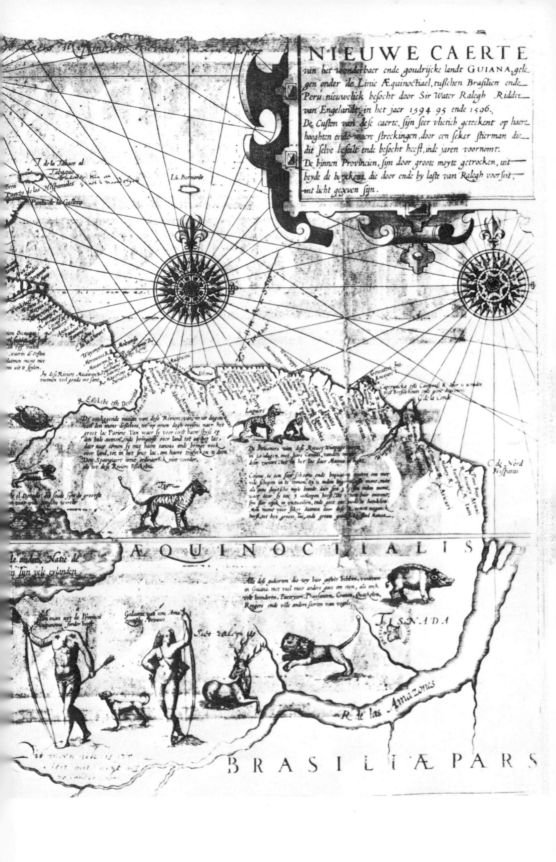

van het wonderbaer ende goudrijcke landt GUIANA, gele-
gen onder de Linie Æquinoctiael, tuffchen Brafilien ende
Peru: nieuwelick befocht door Sir Water Ralegh Ridder
van Engelandt, in het jaer 1594.95. ende 1596.
De Cuften van defe caerte, fijn feer vlietich getreckent op haere
hooghten ende waere ftreckingen, door een feker ftierman die
dit felve befeilt ende befocht heeft, inde jaren voornomt.
De binnen Provincien, fijn door groote moytt getrocken, uit
beyde de bocxkens, die door ende by laft van Ralegh voor feit
int licht gegeven fijn.

ÆQUINOCTIALIS

TISNADA

R. de las Amazones

BRASILIÆ PARS

identified as a member of the chinchilla family, one of the chinchillas or a viscacha, rather than, doubtfully, a raccoon or South American jackal. Another may be an agouti or a paca.

Apart from general appearance, it is likely that the rodents were better known than the carnivores. For one thing they are more diverse, for another they are more likely to be seen than the more nocturnal carnivores and, finally, they are described frequently by the sixteenth century chroniclers whereas the carnivores, apart from jaguar, cougar or puma and local dogs, are mainly ignored.

The peccary, llama, opossum and parrots are still prominent in Le Testu's South America and the country abounds in deer and, with the more usual rhea, has spoonbills (the roseate spoonbill *Ajaia* of the New World) in its avifauna. 'Large birds with beaks like spoons and no tongues' wrote Pigafetta (Robertson 1906).

On an island off South America stands a heavy somewhat indeterminate looking ungulate which might be considered the first appearance of a typical neotropical animal, the tapir. The interpretation may not be correct and the allocation to an island is certainly peculiar but it is possible that this is intended as a tapir and, therefore, precedes other pictorial representations by some forty years. It fits the description given by Enciso 1518 in all respects except that Le Testu's island animal has short ears and in this, too, differs from later pictures. 'And other beastes that be as bigge as an oxe or a cowe and be of grey colour and full of flesshe, ther fete be cloved like the feete of kyne and the hede like the head of a moyl (mule) with long eres, and ther flesshe is very good to ete' (Taylor 1931). The long ears of Enciso's account and later pictures may rule out Le Testu's animal and the tapir may have to wait until the end of the century. But it may be that the exaggerated long ears were themselves a later invention because Fonteneau describes the ears in 1514 only 'aussi grandes que asnes' (Musset 1904). Although Le Testu's animal is not on the mainland of South America, his tapir with its small ears is more realistic than the conventional flop eared animals of the maps at the end of the century.

On his 1566 world map, Le Testu drew only two neotropical land animals and one of these is an armadillo (fig 9.3). Already Desceliers had given one impression of an armadillo, Ribeiro another. But Le Testu's armadillo, probably taken from Belon's *Observations* 1555, bears a close likeness to reality not surpassed until Hondius' 1599 map

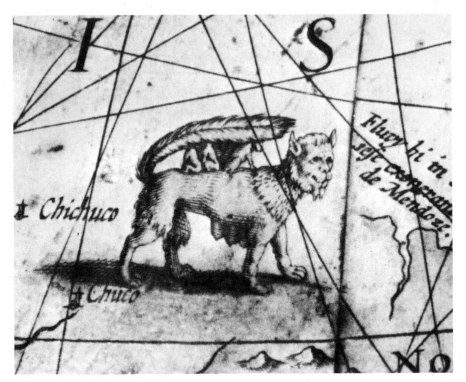

Fig 3.7 The great American anteater on a globe by Hondius 1613 in the
National Maritime Museum, Greenwich

of Guiana copied in de Bry's *America* (fig 3.6).

   More exciting is Le Testu's introduction of another new beast
particular to the neotropical region, the great anteater *Myrmecophaga*
(fig 9.3). The shaggy look, the large tail and the young on its back
make identification with this animal almost certain in spite of the
fact that, in the drawing, it does not have the characteristic long nose
nor fit the description by Oviedo in 1535: 'this beaste (antbeare) in
heare and coloure, is much lyke to the beare of Spayne, and in manner
of the same makynge save that he hath a much longer snout and is of
evyll fyght' (Eden 1555). When it is next depicted on a map, in 1592,
the same animal is described as a dangerous hunting beast, with the
additional information that it carries its young on its back. What is
surprising is that on this 1592 map of Petrus Plancius (Wieder 1925)
it is drawn almost as an inset in the far north of Canada and yet when
it next appears, on an anonymous map of the New World of the late
sixteenth century (Caraci 1927), it has returned to its original position

Fig 3.8 Map of South America by van Langeren for Linschoten's 1595 *Itinerario*: tapirs, howler and opossum in Peru

in South America and stays there for the rest of the century. At the beginning of the following century it makes two expeditions to North America, on an unnamed world map of 1610 in Paris and on a 1613 Hondius globe preserved in Greenwich (fig 3.7) and later returns once more to the south on a 1626 map in Speed's *Prospect of the Most Famous Parts of the World* and stays there through the various editions of the Mercator-Hondius and Blaeu atlases.

On the Petrus Plancius printed map of 1592 there appears another animal that is frequently repeated and possibly made its first appearance on the Ribeiro map of 1529. This is the animal that is said never to eat or drink but to live on air and roar. With a monkey face, it has a carnivore's body and a long striped tail. It seems reasonable to equate this thunderer with the howler monkey *Alouatta* which, according to Antony Knivet describing the fauna of Brazil in 1601, are 'munkies called by the Indians wariva, they are as bigge as a water

Dogge, all blacke, their faces like a man, they have long broad Beards, you shall see twentie of them together in a Tree, and one of them will walke up and downe alwaies with his hand on his Beard making a great noise, and all the rest sitting still and harkening for the space of an houre' (Purchas 1625). This howl has been described in a recent publication: 'they sound like the roll of distant thunder preceded by the death-agonies of half a dozen tortured jaguars' (Sanderson 1955).

Howlers are another variety of cebid monkeys that belong to the neotropical region, their bearded faces, long prehensile tail, comparatively heavy build and trundling progression, with the boney sound-box for howling, differentiate them from their relatives, spider monkeys, douroucoulis, sakis. The beard, the tail and the heavy build are depicted in the drawings of these animals marking them off from the slender cebids of earlier years and then the matter is clinched in the 1598 edition of Linschoten's *Itinerario* when an inscription on the map describes their noise.

The maps of the world, as distinct from the regional maps in the various editions of Linschoten's *Itinerario*, are decorated in the corners with regional fauna. Thus, in such a drawing round the Plancius world map of 1594, tapirs make their first definite appearance, after the less certain representation by Le Testu 1555. The following year, the tapirs have found their way on to van Langeren's map of South America, in a later edition of the *Itinerario* (Bagrow 1964). By now, they have acquired the characteristic described by Enciso, long ears (fig 3.8). Although tapirs had been described by Enciso at the beginning of the century and again by Acosta 'tapirs, which lack horns resemble small mules the skin of these is very precious for leather and other covering, for it is very strong and resistant to blows and shots' (1589), it is not surprising that they had been slow to appear on the maps. Unlike the opossums, monkeys, rodents and armadillos, they are not spread uniformly over the South American and Central American continent nor have they been domesticated like the llamas. There are two types of neotropical tapir, neither of which has floppy ears but ears of reasonably large size and, although they have hoofed feet, they are not, in fact, related to the cloven hoofed animals. They have four hoofs on each front foot and five on each back foot with the axis of symmetry running down the third digit, a feature that allies them to the rhinoceroses and horses. The mountain tapir is confined to the Andes and occurs in

Peru in which position it first occurs on the map. The other South American and Central American tapirs are mainly forest living and shy. Tapirs, then, would not become well known until South America had been explored inland. The third tapir, the only other living representative of the family, occurs in Malaya. There are no tapirs on any other continent and they do not appear on maps anywhere but in South America except the island form of Le Testu.

In 1587, the *Livre de la Marine* of the Pilote Pasterot, in the British Museum, provided an atlas of pen and ink sketches in the Dieppe map tradition, mainly of the southern parts of the world, richly decorated with plants and animals. The now usual parrots, rheas, monkeys, llamas, deer, rabbits or viscachas, peccaries and domestic animals with some possible flying squirrels and quail occupy several maps of parts of South America and a dubious southern continent south of the Straits of Magellan. To these are added a giraffe, several versions of unicorn and some elephants. This is one of the few flagrant deviations from reality. Curiously, although giraffes and unicorns are scattered indiscriminately round the world, there is, nevertheless, a quite diagnostic fauna in South America and in the other regions of the *Livre de la Marine*.

Throughout this later part of the sixteenth century, although new animals were being added to the maps, the tendency was to draw maps without animals. Apart from the *Livre de la Marine*, only a small proportion of the maps of this period contain animals. Those that do continue to depict the neotropical region mainly by armadillos, opossums, llamas and the howler monkey.

The opossum recurs more frequently than any other South American animal, being copied over and over again from Waldseemüller's map and, gradually, becoming less and less like the original, even losing its pouch and only retaining the symbol of the mammary glands with suckling young and the sharp vulpine nose. The howler monkey, too, degenerates to such an extent that it even loses its tail on one map, the tail that had been so prominently featured originally.

Of the birds, the macaws retain their early popularity together with the later arriving rheas and, in 1593, de Jode pictures a toucan (fig 3.9). A toucan beak had been drawn by Belon in 1555 in *L'histoire de la nature des oyseaux*: 'bec d'un oyseau aquatique apporté des terres neufes.' The same beak but with a toucan body attached was figured by Gesner in *de Avibus* in 1585. In 1608, on a Hondius map of the world, belonging to the Royal Geographical Society (Heawood 1937), there appears a penguin and several toucans. It is curious that the appearance of penguins on the maps had been so long delayed for they had been described by some of the earliest voyagers to the Magellan Straits. Pigafetta, accompanying Magellan on his first voyage to the Straits, had reported: 'Truly the great number of these geese cannot be reckoned; in one hour we loaded the five ships. Those geese are black and have all their feathers alike both on body and wings. They do not fly and live on fish. Their beak is like that of a crow' (Robertson 1906). Only a few years later, Andres de Urdaneta reported 'so many ducks without wings that we could not break through them' (Markham 1911). Penguins and toucans reappear, from time to time, on later maps.

Strangely, what appears to be, unequivocally, a turkey, seen from behind, appears on W. J. Blaeu's map of 1618 (Heawood 1943) and is repeated by him in 1631 and later maps. The turkey does not occur wild south of Honduras, being a native of the northern part of the New World, to which it is confined. Occupying a somewhat similar niche in South America are the curassows, whose descriptions have been confused with those of turkeys. The early seventeenth century Dutch cartographer may have been confused with curassows or may have taken for granted the occurrence of turkeys in South America, when they had been so much commented on by the chroniclers of the southern lands of the United States.

On a 1648 world map (Wieder 1925), Joan Blaeu figures a much improved version of an anteater. It had lost its young from its back but it had gained the long nose and long tongue that, together with the huge clawed front feet and bushy tail, make it outstanding in appearance. Other good anteaters occur on Valk's *Nova et Accurata Totus Americae Tabulae* of 1654 (Valk 1680). The South American animals, in general, had ceased to be slavish copies of the Plancius and earlier mapmakers, taking on new life momentarily. Blaeu draws a new and moderately adequate llama, a good armadillo and some sort of iguanid lizard to accompany his anteater.

Fig 3.9 (over) Map of Brazil and Peru in de Jode's *Speculum Orbis Terrae* 1593: howler monkey and opossum in Chile; peccary, toucan, deer and rheas in Brazil

F

BRASILI

Ad Strenuū et Magnificū Dñ
Maiesᵗ & Reuerediſſ. Principi, F

AEQVINOCTI

MARE

Inſulę incognitę

Tropicus Capri.

corni.

PACI

FIC

Chaſdia ſeu Auſtralis Terra,
quā nautarum vulgus Terra
di Fuego vocant, alÿ Pſittacerū
Terram.

PERVVIA.

boricu Echter a Meßpelbrū, Sac.Cas.
poteſi, primū a conſiliis. &c.

Ius. de Cabo
Verde

ALIS.

ERV

BR

A

PICORA

SILI

Braſiliæ populi Toupinanbaulti tel

VIA. CHARCA

Par ana

A.

Acutia.

CHI

Morpion

LI.

Rio de la Plata

CHI

CA

Braſiliæ populi, certis anni
temporibus, ſcaphis ad expe
ditione preparatis, ſe inuice
iuxta littus adoriūtur.

Eſtrecho de la
Victoria.

Eſtrecho de Fernando
Magallanes.

Oriens.

Fig 3.10 Jaguar, capybara and tapir on a map of Brazil in Allardt's *Atlas Major* 1710

By the end of the seventeenth century, animals, if they occur on maps at all, are used decoratively, in cartouches. The macaw retains its symbolism, even through these.

The history of zoogeography, on maps, is virtually at an end with the Coronelli atlases and globes, which leave much to be desired for accuracy, repeating the grave error, for the second time, of putting an elephant into South America (Coronelli 1691–1696). In 1710, C. Allardt has a fine jaguar, tapir and unmistakable capybara on a map of Brazil in his *Atlas Major* and, in 1706, the world map of de Costa e Miranda (in the Mitchell Library, Sydney, Australia) figures armadillo, goat and monkey (fig 9.4).

But, by the end of the seventeenth century, cartographers were concentrating on other things than faunal features, to the evident relief of many of their modern counterparts: 'Delisle's maps (1700) are not outstanding in their execution, but they are free of the mythical monsters and other devices with which the older cartographers had disguised their ignorance—or attracted their customers' (Crone 1953).

SUMMARY OF THE MAP FAUNA

Taking stock of the map fauna, the neotropical region is reasonably complete in respect of mammals. Not only have some five families of unique mammals been recognised (cebid monkeys, anteaters and several rodents) but also two families of birds (rheas and toucans) have been recorded. Furthermore, typical though not restricted mammals have occurred in abundance as well as macaws, penguins and, among reptiles, alligators, iguanas and tortoises. Of the thirty one families of land mammals (excluding bats) occurring in the neotropical region at least fourteen, forty five per cent, are represented on maps.

During the two centuries after the discovery of the New World, the knowledge of the fauna grew and this increase in knowledge is well recorded on the maps. To the early macaws and cebid monkeys, the maps added an opossum in 1516, a rhea in 1527, howler monkey, armadillo and several neotropical rodents in 1529. Guanacos arrived in 1540, iguana in 1541, peccary in 1546, pacos in 1551, anteater in 1566, toucan in 1593, a definite tapir in 1595 (although it had probably occurred already in 1566), a penguin in 1608 and a capybara in 1673.

On the whole, the maps agree with the reports of the naturalists and early travellers who described the South American fauna. There is generally a time lag between the reports of a new animal and its occurrence on a map: Vincent Pinzon described the opossum in 1499 (Ogilby 1671) and it was seventeen years before Waldseemüller included it in the South America of his world map. But, by the end of the sixteenth century, when what might be called the then definitive fauna of the neotropical region was compiled, by Acosta, a large proportion of the animals he described had occurred on maps.

Curiously, it is difficult to identify either a marmoset, a sloth or a porcupine on the maps. Pigafetta had described marmosets, 'little monkeys that look like lions, only yellow and very beautiful' (Robertson 1906) and John Wilson in 1606 described 'monkies . . . which sorts are called Marmosites, and great red ones as bigge as Baboones (those the Indians doe kill and eate) [probably howlers] and there are Leopards [jaguars], and Porcupines, and Lyons [pumas] . . .' (Purchas 1625).

Vasquez de Coronado had recorded porkespicks in 1540 (Hakluyt 1598) but the porcupines may not have been considered worthy of representation as, according to Francis Cooke in 1601, 'Canduaca [coendou] is the porcupine of Africa' (Purchas 1625), an error only cleared up in 1950 (Wood).

Oviedo 1535 had described sloths in detail: 'And in the toppes of theyr neckes, they have verye round faces much lyke unto owles: And have a marke of theyr owne heare after the maner of a cyrcle which maketh theyr faces seeme sumwhat more longe than large. They have smaule eyes and rounde: And nostrylles lyke unto munkeys. They have lyttle mouthes, and move thyr neckes from one syde to an other as thoughe they were astonyshed' (Eden 1555).

Through all these increases in knowledge, the first two animals to depict the neotropical region, recur over and over again: the macaws, dating from 1502 and making what is possibly their last appearance on a cartouche in Kitchin's *New Universal Atlas* in 1794 and the cebid monkeys, dating from 1513 and surviving to appear in a cartouche of Jeffrys in 1776.

The most abundantly filled maps of the region are the South America of Ribeiro's world map of 1529 and the South America of Blaeu's world map of 1618.

Few mistakes had been made through the years by the insertion of animals foreign to the continent: Drake's and Pasterot's unicorns are mistaken in this respect and Pasterot's and Coronelli's elephants and Pasterot's giraffe are even more spectacular mistakes; but Desceliers' mistakes, winged reptiles and four legged rheas, are mistakes of imaginative reconstruction rather than misplacements.

Thus, from a study of pictorial maps, a clear picture can be built up of the mammalian fauna of the neotropical region. It is a fauna that has resulted from a comparatively simple geological history.

ORIGIN OF THE NEOTROPICAL FAUNA

During the early years of the cenozoic period of geological time, some seventy million years ago, South America was separated by sea from North America (Harrington 1962). It is thought that, at that time, the marsupial ancestors of modern opossums and caenolestids and the paleanodont ancestors of armadillos, anteaters and sloths (edentates) crossed the water gap along chains of islands to occupy the southern continent, together with other animals that are no longer represented in the fauna (Darlington 1965). It is possible that the ancestral rheas, toucans and humming birds were also members of this early fauna. These animals evolved isolated from the north, the edentates, for instance, radiating out into many types of armadillos and, eventually, into the sloths and anteaters. Some million years later, across the water, probably still helped by island chains, ancestors of rodents came to found a group of families of neotropical rodents, which includes the hutias, capybaras, viscachas, chinchillas, maras, porcupines and guinea pigs. A little later, the arrival of small arboreal primates founded the marmoset and cebid monkey families (Simpson 1950).

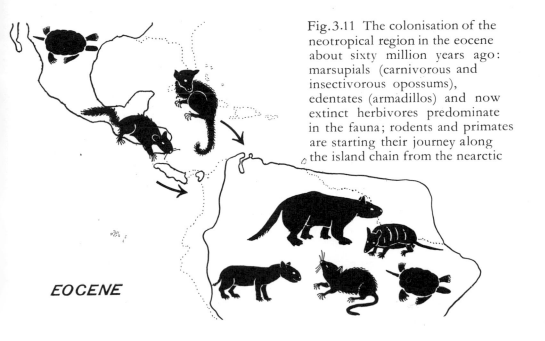

Fig.3.11 The colonisation of the neotropical region in the eocene about sixty million years ago: marsupials (carnivorous and insectivorous opossums), edentates (armadillos) and now extinct herbivores predominate in the fauna; rodents and primates are starting their journey along the island chain from the nearctic

EOCENE

Only by the end of the pliocene, a mere two or three million years ago, were the two continents of the New World rejoined. Peccaries, llamas, tapirs, deer, rabbits, pumas and jaguars were able to get in while, migrating north, armadillos and opossums were able to get out. Much of the ancient neotropical fauna was eliminated at this time, as the continent became colonised from the north, leaving only the edentates, monkeys, rodents and two families of marsupials to mix with the northern forms. Of these northern forms, the tapirs and llamas eventually became extinct in the north, leaving the comparatively recent neotropical versions as their only representatives in the New World, separated from their nearest relatives, the tapir of Malaya and the camel of Bactria, by thousands of miles of apparently uncongenial country.

The maps represent a good proportion of the original neotropical fauna and of the interesting later migrants and, thus, can fairly be said to reflect the unique composition of this fauna; a fauna of birds, lizards, snakes, llamas, monkeys, opossums, peccaries, jaguars, strange rodents and, even stranger, armadillos, anteaters and tapirs.

IV

Nearctic Region

The continent of North America, as far south as central Mexico and as far north as the ice of Canada and including Greenland, is known to zoologists as the nearctic region, the northerly part of the New World. It is a mainly temperate region, lying between the tropics of the New World and the other mainly temperate region, the palearctic, the northerly part of the Old World. Thus, sandwiched between two continents, the nearctic shares its fauna to some extent with both its neighbours. Being temperate and having had closer and more frequent physical connexions with its temperate neighbour, it has greater affinities with the palearctic than with tropical South America. A complex of Old World temperate and New World tropical, the nearctic also has peculiarities of its own. Not as rich in endemic families as the neotropical, it yet has four families of mammals, one of birds and several turtle and amphibian families considered typical nearctic animals (Darlington 1957, George 1962).

THE FAUNA

Of the mammals, the ungulate pronghorns, or American antelope, and the mountain beavers are confined within the boundaries of the region, while pocket mice and pocket gophers, which are primarily indigenous to the region, straggle down into central America, just over the borders of the neotropical region (Hall & Kelson 1959). Three of these typical families are western forms and, superficially, not very different from Old World animals. The pronghorns (Antilocapridae) would be passed off as antelopes or gazelles similar to those from the Old World, the mountain beavers (Aplodontidae) were probably not seen and the pocket mice (Heteromyidae) would be just mice. They would not, therefore, be familiar to the early explorers or the cartographers and they do not play any significant part in the development of faunal map knowledge. The gophers (Geomyidae), though more widely distributed and occurring patchily in the south-east, are not recognisable on maps, although they can be found in written descriptions as early as 1579. On the west coast of North America, Drake observed '. . . great numbers of species of rabbit about the size of a Barbary rat; their tails like that of a rat, and their feet like the paws of a mole. Under their chins on each side they have a bag into which they gather their meat when their bellies are full, to feed their young, or serve themselves another time' (Burney 1803–1817).

Turkeys extend southwards but are outstandingly typical of the North American continent and considered by some to be more suitable as an emblem for the USA than the bald eagle.

It is not, however, these restricted animals that first appear in the drawings of the mapmakers but representatives of some of the other twenty families of mammals that inhabit the nearctic. In contrast to the neotropical, there seems at first to be an emphasis on the similarity of the nearctic animals with those of the Old World which, considering the general similarity of the regions, is not surprising.

THE DISCOVERY OF THE FAUNA

About AD 1000, Leif Eiriksson sailed to the coast of North America and discovered Helluland, which has been interpreted variously as Labrador and Baffin Island. He found, according to the saga of Eirik the Red, that 'there were large numbers of arctic foxes there too . . . and found a land heavily forested, with many wild animals. Offshore to the south-east lay an island. They killed a bear on it' (Jones 1961).

Representatives of two widespread families, the bear and the dog family were, thus, the first to be mentioned as specific of the northern part of the New World and, more important, it seems possible that the foxes were recognised as being particularly northern forms, although nothing is written about their colour.

Nothing further occurs until a few years after the discovery of South America when voyagers, exploring the North Atlantic islands, touched the continent of North America again (Williamson

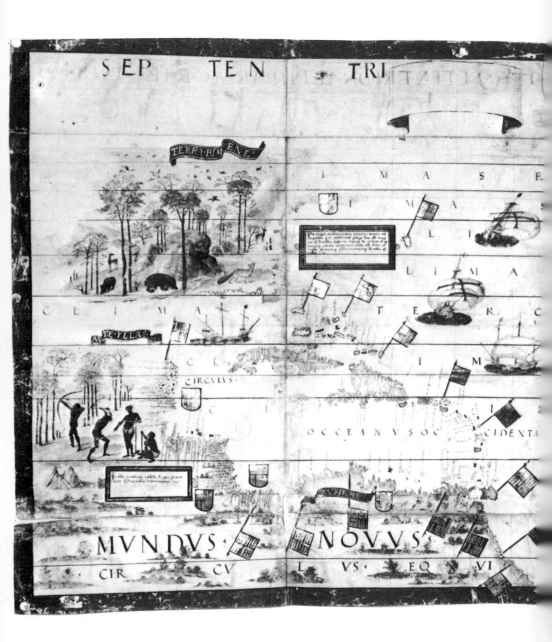

Fig 4.1 Homem-Reinel map of the Atlantic Ocean about 1519 from the Miller Atlas in the Bibliothèque Nationale, Paris: deer, bears, birds and a fox or coyote in North America; deer in Greenland; grey parrots and monkeys in Africa

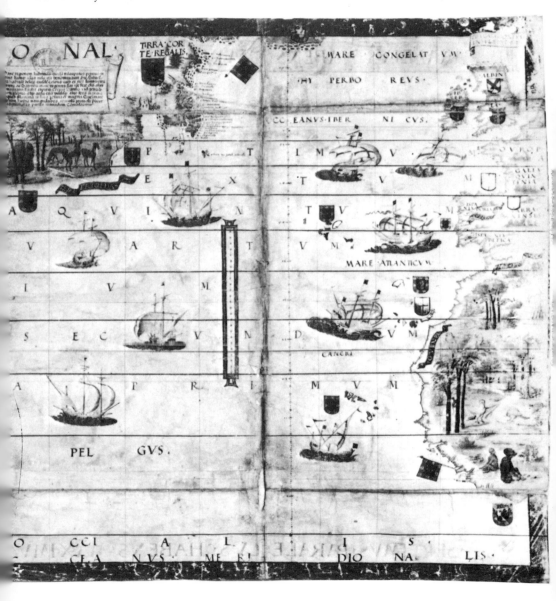

1962). Cabot landed in Newfoundland in 1497 and Corte Real in Labrador in 1500. Both these travellers left brief records of what they saw of the fauna. Both were impressed by large stags with long hair (probably caribou *Rangifer*) and with the numbers of dark coloured falcons, possibly peregrine falcons *Falco peregrinus*. Cabot recorded other birds such as partridges as well as white bears and immense quantities of fish while Corte Real reported (according to the Cantino map 1502) the existence of deer, wolves, foxes, tigers and sables: 'There are very large stags with long hair, the skins of which they use for clothes, and make houses and boats of them. There are also wolves, foxes, tigers [cougars or lynx *Felis concolor* or *Lynx canadensis*] and sables. They affirm that the peregrine falcons are so numerous that it appears to me to be a miracle, like those in our country' (Markham 1893).

Only a short time after these reports were available, indications of a northern continental coastline began to appear regularly on maps, that of Juan de la Cosa in 1500 for example (Nunn 1934). De la Cosa's map is known to be based on the reports of Cabot's voyage but on second hand reports through the Spaniards. It is, therefore, not surprising that no animals are represented on the coasts of North America. Similarly, the Contarini world map of 1506 (Bagrow 1964) was based on reports of Cabot's discoveries that had become known in Venice. Again, there were no animals in the new found land. Not surprisingly, it seems that information about the flora and fauna of a new land was slower to spread than the reports of the land itself or its coastline but see p. 208. It was not until many years later that the first animals appeared.

In 1519, the Homem-Reinel manuscript *Miller Atlas* of the countries of the world (Cortesão and Texeira da Mota 1960) shows a sample of the animals recorded previously (fig 4.1). On the map of the Atlantic Ocean there appear, in the nearctic region, bears (not white), a pale coloured carnivore, many birds that are not easy to identify, deer that are almost certainly red deer *Cervus* (called wapiti in the USA) since the females are shown without antlers.

Whether the carnivore is to be interpreted as fox, wolf or coyote is difficult to decide from the pictures. The early travellers refer to both wolves and foxes and a Spanish map border in 1757 has on it a drawing similar to these small carnivores that run through two centuries of nearctic maps and the animal is labelled coyote (Vindel

1955). Descriptions of the dogs and wolves of the North American
continent make a point of stressing the fact that the dogs do not bark
but howl, again lending support to its interpretation as a coyote.

Bears, coyotes and deer occur more frequently than any other
mammals on North American maps. There is little increase in the
map fauna beyond these three during the first half of the sixteenth
century, in spite of Cabot and Cartier early reporting that, for instance, the bears and other animals in the north were white. Oviedo
added gryfes, or eagles, to the fauna.

The legend on Sebastian Cabot's engraved world map 1544, referring to the voyage of his father to North America in 1497, reads:
'This land is very sterile. There are in it many white bears, and very
large stags, like horses, and many other animals. And in like manner
there are immense quantities of fish soles, salmon, very large cods,
and many other kinds of fish. They call the great multitude of them
baccallos; and there are also in this country dark-coloured falcons
like crows, eagles, partridges, sandpipers, and many other birds of
different kinds' (Jomard 1854). Figured on the map are blue bears,
that could represent either white polar bears, since they are shown in
the north, or the commoner black bears.

The tiger, already referred to by Corte Real, appears on the map.
It is spotted like a jaguar, it is in the south and the jaguar is universally
known as el tigre. Formerly, it ranged at least as far north as Texas.
But, as it occurs in the narratives of those who were further north,
it is perhaps more likely to be the cougar, or mountain lion which,
though usually uniform, has many colour varieties and has distinctly
spotted young. It seems unlikely that this animal can be attributed to
the genus *Lynx*, a suggestion put forward above in interpreting not
a drawing but the Cantino map description. Its long tail and round
ears are not characteristic of lynxes. Jaguar or cougar, it occurs
frequently on later maps, sometimes spotted, sometimes plain and
runs through travellers' tales. Martin Pring commented from Virginia
in 1600 'some say tigers' (Purchas 1625) and Sir John Hawkins commented from Florida in 1565 'probably lions and tigers' (Hakluyt
1598) while the Frenchman René Laudonnière, in the same part of
the continent, observed 'a certaine kinde of beast that differeth little
from the lyon of Africa' (Hakluyt 1598).

The first unambiguous North American polar bear occurs in 1550,
when Desceliers, following the 1534 diary of Jacques Cartier (Biggar

1926), contrasts a polar bear with a black bear by putting it on an ice floe and leaving it white in colour. A brown bear is seen living among trees on the mainland (fig 4.2).

By this time, the middle of the sixteenth century, the more southerly part of the northern continent was becoming known and being represented with more accuracy on the maps. By 1546 Desceliers on one of his earlier maps had drawn a peccary and a porcupine in the nearctic, both being animals shared with the neotropical; the peccary, originally a North American form that migrated to South America after the pliocene; the tree porcupine, a neotropical rodent that migrated north somewhat later. On his 1550 map, Desceliers depicted a turkey for the first time.

From then on, to 1683 on a map of Danckerts (Skelton 1952), the turkey recurs frequently as typical of the nearctic scene. 'But this country abounds chiefly in Turkies, whose plenty deserves no less admiration than their bulk' (Topsell 1658). The turkey is the only unique North American animal that is used with any regularity to depict the nearctic.

Ribeiro, in 1527, figured, for the first time, large birds that continue on the maps as favourite nearctic animals. They are referred to by the explorers by several names, but mainly designated cranes: '. . . such a flocke of cranes (the most part white) arose under us' reports an anonymous writer in 1584 recorded by Hakluyt 1598. They may be flocks of the common egret *Casmerodius albus* or, possibly, even whooping cranes *Grus americana*, all members of wide ranging families with relatives in the Old World. In the 1635 Blaeu *Nouvel Atlas*, two different types of large bird are represented: from their stance, one pair being probably egrets and the other possibly whooping cranes (fig 4.3). Pasterot maps of 1587 add a snipe and a heron.

Then, in 1556, rabbits appear on Gastaldi's map of New France (Nordenskiöld 1897), rabbits listed by Cartier and described for instance by Thomas Hariot, visiting Virginia in 1586: 'those that we have seene, and all that we can heare of are of a gray colour like unto hares; in some places there are such plenty that all the people of some townes make mantles of the furre or glue of the skinnes of those

Fig 4.2 Part of North America from Desceliers' map of the world of 1550 in the British Museum, London: black bear on the mainland, polar bears on ice floes

which thay usually take' (Hakluyt 1598). Although today the jack
rabbit *Lepus townsendii* or *californicus* is a central and western type it is
still such a conspicuous feature of the environment that it is likely
that it fits the description and the pictures on the map better than the
cottontail rabbits, for instance, and might be presumed to have had a
wider range previously. The rabbits continue to be characteristic of
nearctic maps.

With very long eared rabbits, there appear on Sancho Gutiérrez'
map of 1551 deer, quail-like birds, a probable cougar and, possibly
for the first time, bison. The only earlier bison is, very dubiously, the
tapaca of Desceliers' 1546 map. The bison *Bison* (Bovidae), herds of
which were so characteristic of the northern plains until recently,
occurs only sporadically on the maps.

THE DEFINITIVE MAP FAUNA

In 1635, in W. J. Blaeu's *Nouvel Atlas*, the northern continent
becomes colonised by what might almost be called its definitive
fauna, since these particular animals were copied over and over
again on maps of the century. As well as the bears, deer, foxes,
turkeys, egrets, cranes and rabbits that had already been depicted,
Blaeu gave to the nearctic the first beavers and polecats, as well as an
otter with a fish in its mouth. Beavers then become established indicators of the nearctic fauna, interesting in that they belong to a family
of rodents, Castoridae, that occur only in the two northern regions of
the world, the nearctic and the palearctic.

The animals of Blaeu's *Nouvel Atlas* correspond reasonably well
with Cartier's list of Canadian animals written in 1534–1536: white
bears, bears, deer, otters, beavers, martens, foxes, wild cats, hare,
rabbits, squirrels, large muskrats; 'rats sauvaiges, qui vont on l'eaue,
et sont groz comme conninz, et bons à merveilles à menger' (Biggar
1926). Seventy years later, John Smith had only added opossums,
flying squirrels, weasels and minks to this list (Purchas 1625). Squirrels,
flying squirrels and muskrats are frequently written about but only
the tree squirrels have been identified on maps of the nearctic:
Allardt's 1665 map of New Belgium and New England in *Atlas
Major* 1710. The only possible flying squirrels of maps are those of
one of the Pasterot maps and they are shown in South America which
is far south for this genus. The southern flying squirrel extends only
into central America. But the *Compleat Geographer*, Moll, writes in

1723: 'The strange ones unknown to us, are the flying squirrel, so call'd, because it has a fleshy substance like Wings, which it extends, and by the Help of it skips from Tree to Tree, tho' they be 20 or 30 yards distant . . . The *Mussascus* is a sort of Water-Rat, so call'd because it smells of Musk.'

John Smith had observed of the deer that they were 'nothing differing from ours' (Purchas 1625) but many travellers did not agree that the Virginia deer was the same as an Old World deer. Hariot wrote: 'Deere, in some places there are great store: neere unto the Sea Coast they are the ordinary bignesse of ours in England, and some lesse: but further up into the country, where there is better food, they are greater: they differ from ours only in this, their tailes are longer, and the snags of their hornes looke backward' (Hakluyt 1598).

Thus, already different types of deer had been recognised in addition to the long haired caribou. Probably the deer similar to ours are the wapiti (*Cervus* red deer) while the dissimilar ones are the representatives of the New World Odocoileinae or hollow toothed deer. The white tailed Virginian deer *Odocoileus virginianus* has a longish fluffy tail and the antlers are described in a modern book to 'go first backwards and then forwards with all the tines pointing forwards' (Sanderson 1955). The early representatives on the maps are probably the wapiti, since they are the more northerly deer of North America and the females are without antlers. By the middle of the sixteenth century, it is difficult to identify the type of deer, though some may correspond to the shaggy haired caribou, a larger equivalent of the Old World reindeer and much written about at this period. Le Testu, in *Cosmographie Universelle* 1555, figures large numbers of deer that might be thought to signify variety of genera, some of them having the large ears of the Odocoileinae. By the following century, when the map fauna had in the main come south, the deer take on some of the distinctive characteristics of the southern white tailed deer. They have distinctly white rumps and, although the antlers are formalised into no very obvious pattern, there seems little doubt that they represent the white tailed Virginia deer.

Fig 4.3 (over) The fauna of New Belgium and New England from Blaeu's *Nouvel Atlas* 1635: turkey, beavers, cranes, otter, polecat, egrets, coyotes, deer, rabbits and bears

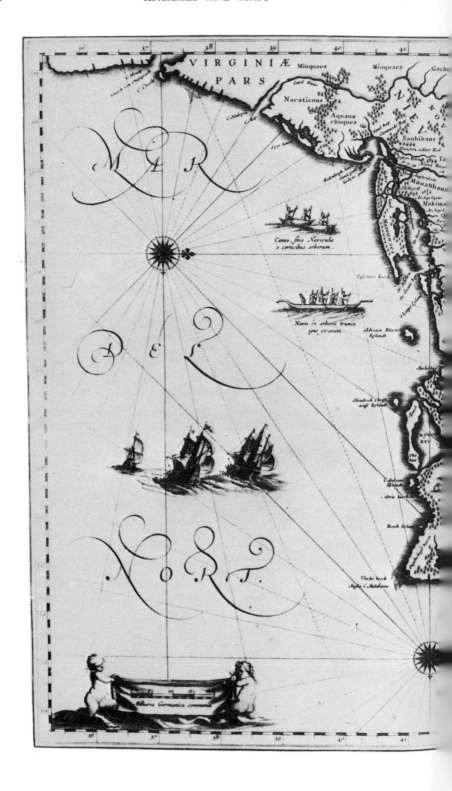

The animals of Blaeu's *Novus Atlas* were copied by Janssonius 1646, by Visscher 1655 and almost certainly by others such as Ferrar 1651 (Skelton 1958), Thorlaksson 1669 (Nørlund 1944), de Wit about 1650, van Keulen 1660, Speed 1676, Morden 1680, Danckerts 1683 (Skelton 1952), Seutter 1740 and Allardt 1710 although there were occasional additions to the Blaeu prototype fauna. In the main, the tendency was increasingly to add domestic animals, epitomized by the groups of horses, cows, pigs, goats and turkeys in Pennsylvania on Danckerts' map of New Belgium, New England and Virginia in 1683.

A 1665 map in Allardt's *Atlas Major* 1710, the map of New Belgium (fig 4.4), depicts a large and varied fauna including, in addition to Blaeu's basic animals and some domestic varieties, many and various birds among them pheasants, a largely Old World family that extends into the nearctic. The only armadillo of nearctic maps occurs. The nine banded armadillo is the only member of the South American edentate order to have spread to North America and, in the south of the United States, it flourishes. The northerly spread has been particularly rapid during the last hundred years so that, when Allardt's atlas was made, it is unlikely that the armadillo occupied more than the most southern of the middle and western states.

In 1605, on a map of the world, in the possession of the Hispanic Society of the United States, Blaeu had figured an opossum in the nearctic. So, by 1673, the four families that the nearctic shares with the neotropical, the opossum, armadillo, tree porcupine and peccary families had all been represented.

Allardt's 1665 map also has an animal that looks like an antelope. It is of goat build with straight gyred horns. It is just possible that this might be the single representation of the unique nearctic antelope or pronghorn *Antilocapra americana*, but there is no evidence that the animal was known at this time. It was first named in 1818 (Harlan 1825) and so, therefore, judgment must be suspended.

One of the latest maps to be illustrated with the North American fauna was also well populated. This was the map of New York by Seutter, following Visscher, published in 1740 and owned by the New York Historical Society. The surroundings of New York are inhabited by both the commonly known wild animals such as bears, foxes, otters, martens, beavers, rabbits, caribou, deer, turkeys, egrets and the more obviously domesticated goats, cows, pigs and horses.

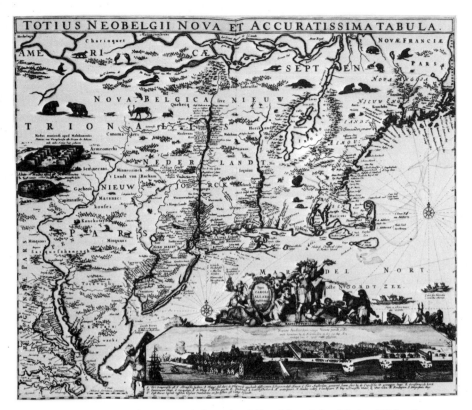

Fig 4.4 1665 map of New Belgium in Allardt's *Atlas Major* 1710: foxes or coyotes, egrets, bears, deer, otter, polecat, beavers, goats, dogs, pheasant, turkeys, rabbits, possible armadillo, antelope or pronghorn, possible raccoon

For the most part, then, the nearctic was represented on pictorial maps by common animals of a temperate region. The likenesses to the Europe, from which the early travellers came, tended to be stressed with deer, bears, beavers and rabbits in particular. The turkey stands alone among the unique animals with the possible exception of the pronghorn.

But, although the North American fauna may not seem to be of outstanding interest on the maps, in its less spectacular way it has contributed almost as much information as the maps of South America. Of the twenty three families of land mammals inhabiting the nearctic region, thirteen definitely appear on the maps, only one less than for the neotropical region, but a larger proportion of the total, fifty six per cent compared with forty five per cent. If the pronghorn is acceptable this puts the number higher.

All four families shared with its southerly neighbour are illustrated; but only one, the beavers, of the four palearctic families shared. It is not surprising that moles and jumping mice (zapodids) were not considered worthy of illustration and the western pikas were almost certainly either not known or referred to in the all inclusive term of conies. Of the widespread animals three quarters appear on the maps.

It is interesting that few reptiles are figured. One of the most striking differences between the palearctic and the nearctic is the abundance, in the latter, of turtles of many sorts, lizards and, in particular, snakes. Explorers commented on the alligators and one appears on the Coronelli globe of 1688–1696 in the Bibliothèque Nationale in Paris and another in an inset in the *American Atlas* of T. Jefferys 1776. Turtles never appear and yet they are still conspicuous elements of the more southern parts of the region. It is less surprising that salamanders, of which almost all live in the nearctic or palearctic, should not be figured.

With these reservations it can be said, in general, that the maps give an impression of the fauna that is still obtainable today. Bears, deer and jack rabbits are conspicuous. Skunks and ground squirrels, however, that are obvious today, may have then been overshadowed by the bison and beavers, that were then so abundant.

Some maps of North America are more thickly populated with a wide variety of native animals than any other maps of other regions: Allardt's 1665 map of New Belgium is outstanding.

ALIENS

In contrast to South America, the North American maps have a range of obvious aliens within their borders.

Unicorns appear three times and were also described. Sir John Hawkins reported unicorn horns in Florida in 1565 (probably teeth of the narwhal whale) and, in 1539, Friar Marco de Niça commented: 'Here they showed me an hide halfe as bigge againe as the hide of a great oxe, and told me that it was the skin of a beast which had but one horne upon his forehead, and that this horne bendeth toward his breast, and that out of the same goeth a point right forward, wherein he hath so great strength, that it will break anything how strong so ever it be, if he runne against it, and that there are great store of these beasts in that country. The colour of the hide is of the colour of a great goat-skin, and the haire is a finger thicke' (Hakluyt 1598). This seems to refer to a wild goat, a guess supported by the fact that Desceliers' unicorns have beards. In general, however, it is difficult to account for the presence of these occasional unicorns, because neither the North American deer nor the pronghorns have the straight horns of some of the Old World antelopes, that could have been mistaken for unicorns. Only the North American goat-antelopes *Oreamnos* seem likely to be seen in profile as having a single un-branched horn. These animals, however, are confined to the mountains of the west. But, goat-like the nearctic unicorns seem to be, bearded, with unbranched horn and, according to Friar Marco, with the horn curving downwards and forwards.

Of the other aliens, Gastaldi, in *L'Universale Orbe della Terra* 1550, depicts, among common animals, elephants and a dragon, across a land occupying what is now known to be the sea of the Bering Straits (Grande 1905). There are the unexplained northern appearances of anteaters, in 1592 on the world map of Plancius (Wieder 1925), on the 1610 anonymous world map in Paris and on the 1613 Hondius globe in Greenwich. In 1569, Camocio, on a map of the world, notable for fantasy rather than accuracy, put a rhinoceros and a camel in Canada. In 1587, one of the North American maps, in Pasterot's atlas, has a giraffe.

The elephants, rhinoceroses, camel and giraffe of the nearctic are, perhaps, the most important aberrations in animal mapmaking and, as exceptions, merit the scorn that has been poured wrongly on cartographic animals in general. Even so, these animals were not, in fact, mythical, but put in the wrong places for no apparent reason except, possibly, as has often been suggested, to fill the gaps. But they may be being used as indicators of the presence, in what were mainly unexplored territories, of many unfamiliar animals.

V

Palearctic Region

The other great north temperate zoogeographical region of the world is the palearctic, whose boundaries are less obvious than those of the New World regions. The palearctic runs south as far as the Sahara desert in Africa, takes in a corner of Arabia and then skirts the Himalayas, running to the China coast just south of the lowlands of China and south of Japan.

DEFINITION OF THE REGION

For the present purpose, in eastern Asia a guess has had to be made as to whether the animals are intended to be north or south of the boundary line and the north coast of Africa and the greater part of Arabia has been excluded from the palearctic region and considered to lie within the ethiopian region. This has not obscured the situation to the extent that might be expected. Rather the reverse, since the commonest animals depicted in northernmost Africa are, in fact, the camels with the occasional ostrich and elephant. As has already been seen, the camels are palearctic animals by origin, ostriches are known to have lived a good deal further north in historic times than they do today and the elephants, as domestic animals, have been spread considerably by man.

Taking, then, a slightly restricted view of the palearctic, limited to Europe and northern Asia, on maps the most commonly occurring animals are the various sorts of deer, followed by camels, bears, feline carnivores of various kinds and, mainly domesticated, horses. These representatives of the palearctic carry on the tradition of camel, lion and reindeer from the maps of the earlier centuries. As on the maps of North America, there is a tendency in the seventeenth century to portray more domestic animals in this northern part of the world: horses, sheep and cattle are frequent and parallel their nearctic relatives. However, the goat, obviously domesticated, equally obviously wild in other cases, occurs as frequently as other bovids. In this, the palearctic differs from the nearctic in the cartographers' hands and conforms to reality.

DEER

Deer are frequent in the palearctic and, in scattering them across the maps, the cartographers have indicated both the variety of species and their common occurrence throughout the north temperate lands. They are not restricted to this region, being common in the nearctic and oriental and occurring, also, in the neotropical region. The maps of the nearctic and the neotropical have already been shown to have representatives of the cervid family on them, more frequently in the north than in the south. But the cartographers have indicated more variety in the palearctic than in any other region. This is not unreasonable, since the deer are a predominantly northern family and the palearctic has twice as many genera as the nearctic.

From the earliest maps, three types of deer are common in the palearctic: the three that the palearctic shares with the nearctic and which have been seen to occur from time to time on nearctic maps. These three are the elk *Alces* (called moose in the USA), the reindeer *Rangifer* (called caribou in the USA) and the red deer *Cervus* (called wapiti in the USA). These continue to be the favourites of the cartographers, until they are joined in the sixteenth century by fallow deer *Dama* and, in the seventeenth century, by musk deer *Moschus*.

Of these five genera, the elk is the first to appear, on the thirteenth century Ebstorf map (fig 9.3). It is distinguished by the heavy antlers and cloven hoofs and is labelled elkes. Two centuries later, another elk appears, in Europe, from behind some trees on the decorative Borgia map of the world (fig 2.12). There is no mistaking it but it is arguable that it is less satisfactory than the diagrammatic Ebstorf elk, having the tines on the apposing and upper edges of the antlers whereas the Ebstorf elk bears them more accurately on the outer edges. By 1539, on Olaus Magnus's map of Scandinavia the *Carta Marina* (Lynam 1949), the elks have become numerous and their

antlers, still formalised, resemble the Ebstorf elk. In 1550, a somewhat unsatisfactory representation appears on Desceliers' map
(fig 5.1); and it is not until 1578 that something more than a formal
picture occurs, on one of Antony Jenkinson's maps in de Jode's
Speculum Orbis Terrae, where the elk proudly occupies a corner of
Europe (fig 5.2).

The reindeer and the red deer represent the palearctic on the maps
more often than any other animal. 'The reindeer is the size of an ox;
it has branching horns, cloven hooves, and a fleece as shaggy as a

Fig 5.1 Part of Desceliers' 1550 map of the world in the British Museum,
London: elephant, elk and bear in the palearctic region

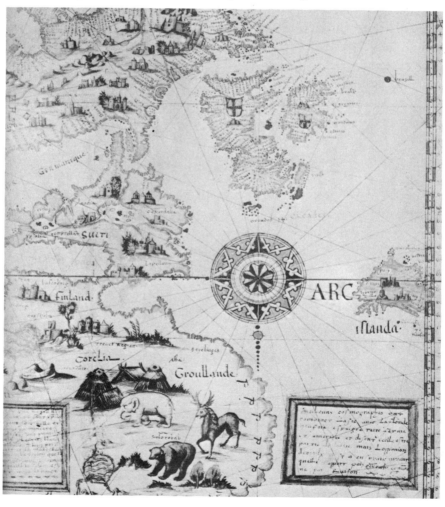

bear's but, when it happens to be self-coloured, resembling an ass's coat. The hide is so hard that they use it for making cuirasses' (Pliny). The reindeer occurs most frequently in domestic roles. On the early Catalan maps of the fourteenth century and maps of the early part of the sixteenth century, reindeer are ridden by falconers in the northern lands, reaching the summit of domestication in 1539, when Olaus Magnus features them abundantly. They are being milked, they draw carts and they are ridden. His description in *Historia de Gentibus Septentrionalibus* 1555 of the many-branched antlers of the 'ranged

Fig 5.2 Elk on a map of Waldeccensis (East Germany) by Antony Jenkinson 1578 from de Jode's *Speculum Orbis Terrae*

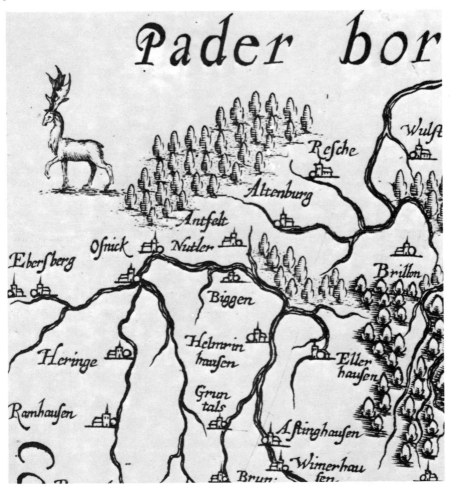

deer called Rangifer' is more detailed than his representation of them on the map. 'Of these horns it hath two bigger than the rest, growing as the stags horns do: but they are with more branches, and farther out, for they augment to fifteen branches. Another stands in the middle of their head, with little small branches shorter than the other, standing about it. These arm the head on all sides against the beasts that are Enemies unto it, especially wolves. . . . It hath a mane like a Horse, and the hoofs are divided in two, being almost round by Nature, because it runs over the high snow, carrying a man on its back, where the snow is hardened in Valleys, Mountains or Fields.' Reindeer continue on the maps, used either for riding or, more usually, harnessed, until their last appearance in 1729 on Bering's map of Siberia (Skelton 1958). Although there is little possibility of mistaking the identity of the animals through the centuries, they are not, in fact, accurately drawn as reindeer, except for those which decorate Anders Bure's Scandinavian map of 1626 (fig 5.3).

Preceding the reindeer in time, the red deer first occur on the Bodleian Library Gough map in 1360. At Colgarth on Loch Ness 'hic maxima venaccio.' The antlers are reasonably well indicated and the animal has cloven feet and a short tail. Red deer, with more or less formalised antlers, prance across many maps during the succeeding centuries, until they are joined by the unadorned female in 1557, J. Franciscum (fig 5.5). After that there is a marked tendency for them to appear in pairs. Their last appearance is in 1706 on the world map of Juan de Costa e Miranda.

Apart from these three common cervid genera, fallow deer are, certainly, represented spotty in 1557 (fig 5.5); and, again, in 1593 by de Jode.

In 1655, as a cartouche in a late edition of Blaeu's *Nouvel Atlas*, a good musk deer represents Tartary and Samarkand (fig 5.4). The musk deer has been known to the west, as an inhabitant of palearctic regions, since it was reported on, in detail, by Marco Polo at the end of the thirteenth century. He reported it to be like a gazelle: 'It has feet and tail like the gazelle's, and stag's hair of a very coarse kind, but no horns. It has four tusks, two below and two above [only two, the upper canine teeth], about three inches long, and slender in form, one part growing upwards, and the other downwards. It is a very pretty creature. The musk is found in this way. When the creature has been taken, they find at the navel between the flesh and

Fig 5.3 Reindeer on *Orbis Arctoi* of Anders Bure 1626

Fig 5.4 Musk deer on the map of Tartary and Samarkand in Blaeu's *Nouvel Atlas* 1655

the skin something like an imposture full of blood, which they cut out and remove with all the skin attached to it. And the blood inside this imposture is the musk that produces that powerful perfume' (Yule & Cordier 1903). The killing of the deer for the sake of its musk has, effectively, reduced its once widespread range. Even at its most successful, during historic times, the musk deer has always been confined to the palearctic.

Thus, five of the eight palearctic genera of the deer family are clearly depicted on the maps.

It is possible that some drawings may have been intended to portray roe deer *Capreolus*: not only on the visual evidence is this suggested but also because roe deer had already been named and occur in the literature. Strabo reported roe deer. Albertus Magnus, for instance, includes the Rehbock in his German fauna and, a near contemporary of it, a woodcut of a roe deer, in Vienna, bears considerable resemblance to the deer on some maps, in the Armenia of the 1504 *Nautical Map of the World* of Maggiolo, in the Biblioteca

Federiciana in Fano, for example. Friar William of Rubruck had also mentioned the occurrence of roe deer in Tartary in 1253 (Hakluyt 1598) although, from the context, these have been interpreted, perhaps more correctly, as gazelles (Rockhill 1900). There seems to have been a general confusion between roes and gazelles which it is difficult to sort out satisfactorily.

Only two genera of deer were completely ignored, Père David's deer *Elaphurus* unknown until 1865 and the little Chinese water deer *Hydropotes* which, if known, may have been confused with the musk deer.

CARNIVORES

To hunt the deer through the temperate lands of the palearctic are the carnivorous felids and canids. Represented as spotted lynxes or cheetahs, as lions, foxes and wolves, they occur on many occasions on palearctic maps. A lion pursues a gazelle in 560 and represents the palearctic on the Vercelli map of the thirteenth century. In 1360, on the Gough map, a wolf inhabits Sutherland to prey on the red deer nearby. Foxes or wolves roam round the Behaim globe in 1492 and the earlier Borgia world map (fig 2.12). A lynx inhabits the Hereford palearctic (fig 2.3). Lynxes leap through Scandinavia in 1539. At this date, too, the first arctic foxes make their appearance, running round an ice-bound Iceland. They appear again, over a century later, in Seller's *English Pilot* in 1671 and, finally, the two colour phases, white foxes and black foxes, are drawn side by side on maps of Siberia drawn for Bering in the years round 1729 and 1735 (Skelton 1958). A white fox and a black (or blue) fox occupy the foreground of a human habitation in Siberia.

Also frequent, from an early date and persisting through the centuries, are the palearctic bears. They first appear on the thirteenth century T-O maps as representative of palearctic regions and continue until the end of the seventeenth century. It is interesting that, although polar bears are depicted earlier on palearctic maps than on nearctic maps, they are not differentiated from other bears as often as on nearctic maps yet they were reported as occurring in the palearctic

Fig 5.5 (over) Part of a map of Palestine by J. Franciscum 1557: two humped camel, spotty fallow deer, red deer, horses, cows, unicorn and snake

as far back, at least, as Albertus Magnus and Marco Polo. 'You find in this country immense bears entirely white, and more than 20 palms in length,' wrote Marco Polo (Yule & Cordier 1903). A polar bear emerges from a lair in Norway on the fifteenth century Borgia map (fig 2.12), goes through many activities in Olaus Magnus's map of Scandinavia 1539, floats on ice until late editions of Ortelius 1590, runs through the arctic regions on Barents' map of northern Norway in Waghenaer 1596 and makes a late appearance, as a cartouche, in the 1680 *Zee-Atlas* of J. van Keulen.

The palearctic has thus been represented most often by the cartographers as a land populated by deer, bears and other more active carnivores. These are animals that have a generally wide distribution round the world and are not confined to the palearctic nor even to the Old World. Felid and canid carnivores are world wide in their distribution although, in a genuinely wild form, they may be absent from Australia and some islands. Bears and deer are more restricted, being absent from the ethiopian and australian regions. They may be regarded as typical north temperate families that have spread south to the New World tropics but, in the Old World, to the tropics of the oriental region only.

OTHER NORTHERN ANIMALS

In contrast to the bears and deer is the horse family. In its wild state it is a family shared only by the ethiopian and palearctic regions. Known fossil until comparatively recent times from the New World, the horses became extinct there and were only later reintroduced by the Spaniards. Herds of horses had been recorded as wild and characteristic of Europe and Asia by Strabo and many of his successors. William of Rubruck saw 'wild asses . . . in great numbers, and these are like mules' (Rockhill 1900) and yet they occur on only a few maps as palearctic wild animals: Anthonius Wied's *Muscovia* 1555 (Nordenskiöld 1897) for example and, in 1578, in Mercator's *Tabulae Geographicae* on two maps of Asia. Similarly, their ethiopian counterpart, the zebra, is only an occasional visitor to African maps. Horses on maps are mainly domestic animals and, as such, are frequent but more widely dispersed.

Entirely different in its distribution round the world is the camel family, which occurs wild in the palearctic and the neotropical

H

regions. Camels are very common on palearctic maps although, mainly, in the one humped domestic version. Occasionally, the Bactrian two humped camel recurs, in the *Cosmographie Universelle* of Le Testu in 1555 and on a map of Palestine by J. Franciscum in 1557, for example (fig 5.5).

Maps, in general, denote the palearctic as a region of deer, camels, bears, hunting carnivores and domestic horses, cattle, sheep and goats with the occasional falcon, pheasant and a rare dragon. In the abundance of cervid, bovid and camelid herbivores and of bears and the smaller carnivores this is not an unreasonable representation, even though none of the families is restricted to the region.

The two unique families of the palearctic are obscure rodents which have only become known to zoologists since long after the last animal decorated maps were produced. Rodents were not, in any case, generally attractive to the cartographers, although they are often mentioned in travellers' narratives. William of Rubruck described the Tartars in 1253: 'they will neither eate mise with long tailes, nor any kinde of mise with short tails. They have also certain lettle beasts called by them sogur, which lie in a cave twenty or thirty of them together, al the whole winter sleeping there for the space of six moneths [marmots] and these they take in great abundance. There are also a kind of conies having long tayles like unto cats; and on the outside of their tailes grow black and white haires [ground squirrels, almost certainly not jerboas as some editors suggest]' (Hakluyt 1598).

It is perhaps surprising that beavers are hardly ever depicted in the palearctic and yet they are a northern rodent family, shared only with the nearctic, where they occur freely on the maps. For, although the beaver has become more and more restricted in the palearctic region since the retreat of the ice at the end of the last glacial epoch and with the advent of civilisation, it had been known and recorded from early times by men of the Mediterranean lands and was always included in the early bestiaries. Herodotus reports a big lake in Scythia where otters and beavers were caught. Aristotle describes how 'the beaver is flatter than the otter and has strong teeth; it often at night time emerges from the water and goes nibbling at the bark of the aspens that fringe the riversides. . . . The hair of the beaver is rough, intermediate in appearance between the hair of the seal and the hair of the deer' (Thompson 1910). Pliny tells the story of the beaver's self mutilation when in danger and adds: 'apart from this the beaver is an animal with a formidable bite, cutting down trees on the river banks as if with steel . . . the beaver has a fish's tail, while the rest of its conformation resembles an otter's; both species are aquatic, and both have fur that is softer than down.' Albertus Magnus rejected the story of self mutilation but, by the time the beaver appeared on the 1539 Scandinavian map of Olaus Magnus, a new legend had been incorporated. Olaus Magnus described the castors 'laying one on its back and piling wood on it and using it as a cart' and they appear in this operation on the map.

THE MAPS OF OLAUS MAGNUS AND ANDERS BURE

Olaus Magnus's woodcut *Carta Marina* 1539 (fig 5.6) with Anders Bure's *Orbis Arctoi Nova et Accurata Delineatio* 1626 (figs 5.3 and 5.7) are outstanding among maps of the palearctic and are confined to Scandinavia. The two maps were not revolutionary from the cartographic point of view but they were outstanding for the full portrayal of the fauna of the regions. Both give a dynamic representation of Scandinavian animals.

In 1539, among the more usual elks, reindeer, lynx, bear, foxes and other small carnivores, Olaus Magnus figures rodents, an order otherwise remarkably absent from maps. Among the rodents is a squirrel, beavers, mountain hares and, probably, mice being eaten by a dragon and by foxes. There is a horse in west Frisia which is not obviously domesticated and there is a picture of the now extinct wild aurochs, in Russia.

The aurochs or wild ox was always confined to Europe and may be the progenitor of most of the modern domestic cattle. It was probably represented on the Hereford thirteenth century map, in Europe, as it had been known and had been named hundreds of years earlier. 'Some remarkable breeds of wild oxen, the maned bison and the exceptionally powerful and swift aurochs, to which the ignorant masses give the name of buffalo, though the buffalo is really a native of Africa and rather bears some resemblance to the calf and stag,' wrote Pliny.

A wild pig storms through White Russia and the lakes are filled with fish of all types. Birds are numerous, from pelicans to many sorts of birds of prey. There are also snakes.

Fig 5.6 Part of the 1572 Lafreri copy of Olaus Magnus's 1539 *Carta Marina*: dragon, reindeer, mountain hares, horses, beavers, gluttons, bears, squirrel, wolves and elk

The number of small carnivores is extended to include otters, a marten, a sable and, most interestingly, the gulones. The occurrence of gulones in 1539, less realistically in the 1572 Lafreri copy of the *Carta Marina*, later on seventeenth century maps (Bure 1626), as well as in cartouches as late as d'Anville's *Nouvel Atlas de la Chine* 1737 and Barnikel's *Ducatus Curlandiae* 1747, is an interesting palearctic phenomenon.

The *Gulo*, wolverine or glutton, related to the badgers, was once more widespread than it is today, ranging over the greater part of North America, Europe and Asia. It is comparatively large, as much as a metre in length and weighing up to twenty kilogrammes. It is aggressive in accordance with its size. It may be Herodotus' 'creature with a square face, whose skin they use for making edges for their jackets; its testicles are good for affections of the womb.' Gulones were reported in 1553, by Sir Hugh Willoughby, as animals of particular interest, being unknown to him from the more southerly and western parts of Europe (Hakluyt 1598). It was probably from direct experience that Olaus Magnus figured them on his map. It was not, by any means, fortuitous that his map was a Scandinavian natural history. He had travelled widely in the north and studied carefully before his map was actually cut in Venice in 1539. With his map is an *Opera Breve* which describes the pictures, pictures not only of animals but of people, activities and historic incidents and, in 1555, he published the *Historia de Gentibus Septentrionalibus* which described both the northern peoples, their occupations and history and the natural history of the area. Of the gulo he wrote: 'The gulo is as a great dog and his ears and face are like a cats: his feet and nails are very sharp: his body is hairy with long brown hair, his tail is like a Foxes, but somewhat shorter, but his hair is thicker, and of this they make brave winter caps.' He goes on to describe, how it eats a carcase until it is bursting and then pushes between two trees to squeeze it out; as such, with little other resemblance to Olaus' description, it appears on his map. Gluttons are reputed to be capable of pulling down deer and it is in this act that one is shown in 1747. The North Americans, equally, had their myths about the gluttons, even though these did not seem to be communicated to the early travellers in those regions and, thus, did not reach the maps as the beavers did. The glutton was an animal much feared by the Eskimos and North American Indians, because of its deceitful nature. But, in myths, it had the reputation of teaching a method of trapping eagles and other animals; a myth based, presumably, on its reputation for stealing traps. 'The glutton is the only member of the weasel family that cannot be trapped. It amuses itself by stealing, not only the animals caught in the traps, but also the traps themselves. The trapper can only get rid of them by shooting' (Brouillette 1934).

The *Carta Marina* is a genuine, though local, distribution map.

Olaus Magnus's map was engraved and reissued by Antonio Lafreri in 1572 and copied many times between then and the next great step in Scandinavian cartography in 1626. The glutton and the other innovations of his map recur sometimes as, for instance, on Waghenaer's *Spieghel de Zeevaerdt* in 1588 and later editions.

In 1626, Anders Bure's *Orbis Arctoi* was issued, in a quite different style from the earlier Olaus Magnus maps. The animals that populate Bure's northern lands are drawn with considerable accuracy. Again, the map represents an essay in animal distribution as well as land distribution. There are both wild and domestic reindeer (fig 5.3), male and female red deer, bear, otters, foxes and goats as well as a stork and what is, probably, a glutton 'with a square face'. Again, strikingly, there are many rodents; this time, distinct mice and many rabbits (fig 5.7). Rabbits had occurred, sporadically, since 1516 on Waldseemüller's *Carta Marina*.

After 1626, animals began to die out from the maps of the palearctic, though persisting sporadically until the early years of the next century. An inset to a map of the Low Countries in Blaeu's 1635 *Nouvel Atlas* is interesting for showing both ibex *Capra ibex* and chamois *Rupicapra rupicapra*, typical wild goats of the palearctic. But, in general, even the animals of the cartouches died out more rapidly from the paleartic than they did from the more romantic, less well known, tropical regions of the world.

STRAYS

The only strays on maps of the palearctic are some northerly Asian rhinoceroses (some Linschoten maps and Blaeu's 1618 world map), three unicorns (Maggiolo 1504, an anonymous Portuguese map in

Fig 5.7 (over) Part of Anders Bure's *Orbis Arctoi* 1626: mice, bear, fox, rabbits or hares, deer, stork, goats and possibly glutton

the Koningklijke Bibliotheek in the Hague about 1540 and Franciscum's 1557 map of Palestine) and several elephants.

The rhinoceroses of the palearctic are found in China and so they
are not, therefore, in terms of animal distribution, very far from
their correct home in the oriental region; so they can be dismissed as
slight inaccuracies.

The unicorns, too, are probably borderline cases, see p.137.

The elephants occur, usually, round the borders of the region and
are not, therefore, seriously misplaced. But Desceliers' 1550 palearctic
elephant (fig 5.1); and the elephant of Oliva portolans of about
1646 (Musée de la Marine, Paris) are exceptions, placed firmly in
Europe. There seems no obvious explanation of these strays nor,
satisfactorily, of the puzzling animal in Scandinavia on the 1516
Waldseemüller *Carta Marina* which is difficult to identify (Bagrow
1964). From Waldseemüller's inscription, it seems to be a wild boar
because of its bite, the crest on its head and the two long squared
tusks. Its heavy build, compared in size with an elephant, makes
such an identification less certain. A similar animal occurs in the
Finland of a Vallard map of 1547 (fig 5.8). It does not add anything to
make the identification easier and is, in any case, probably copied
from Waldseemüller.

THE MAP FAUNA

Thus, although familiar to the cartographers and, therefore, less
exciting from a pictorial point of view, the palearctic acquired a
reasonable fauna through the centuries in spite of the earlier conten-
tions that there were few wild animals in the north (Strabo, for instance) except for ungulates.

In the general absence from the region of flamboyant birds and
of most reptiles, the maps coincide with reality. Neither parrots, nor
any of the flightless large birds occur now in the palearctic and, while
the palearctic may well be the distributive centre of the pheasant
family, the most outstanding members of that family occur in the
oriental region. Storks or cranes appear from time to time on the
maps; there are pelicans in 1539; the occasional ostrich, mainly on
the early maps. Pheasant-like birds appear occasionally, from Ribeiro
1529 to some final cartouches of d'Anville in 1737, but only the birds
of prey persist with any sort of regularity.

The palearctic has a smaller variety of reptiles than any other

Fig 5.8 Unidentified animal in the Finland of the Vallard Atlas 1547 in the Huntington Library, California

region and so, not surprisingly, few are found on maps, though Olaus Magnus figures snakes.

Thus, affinities with its temperate neighbour, the nearctic, are emphasised on the maps, by the presence of various deer in both regions and polar bears, foxes and otters. The occasional horse and the ostriches are a reminder of its affinity with the ethiopian region and its pheasants of its affinity with both the nearctic and oriental regions. The scarcity of reptiles sets it apart as a cool temperate region.

HISTORY OF THE FAUNA

During the seventy million years or so since the end of the mesozoic, the palearctic was joined and severed from the nearctic on many occasions, so that while animals were often free to journey between the two great continents, they were kept separate often enough for a certain amount of differentiation to occur (Simpson 1947). Thus, the palearctic is not identical in its fauna with the nearctic. The palearctic has pigs, the nearctic peccaries; the palearctic mole rats, the nearctic pocket gophers; the palearctic hedgesparrows, the nearctic turkeys. But they share the world's talpid moles, beavers and tailed amphibians, for example.

The palearctic, also, had connexions in the south. It was connected with the oriental region until well on into the cenozoic, the continuity of the two regions being uninterrupted by the present day mountain ranges. It was connected with the ethiopian region until late mesozoic days, lost the connexion and, then, regained it in the middle of the cenozoic (Moreau 1952). The palearctic-oriental connexion provided a land mass which was the main home of pheasants. The palearctic-ethiopian connexion, from the oligocene on-

Fig 5.9 The northern lands in the eocene about sixty million years ago: ancestral rhinoceros in the palearctic left centre and ancestral carnivores left centre and bottom centre; camel and ungulate in the nearctic right centre; primates, insectivores and marsupials common to both regions

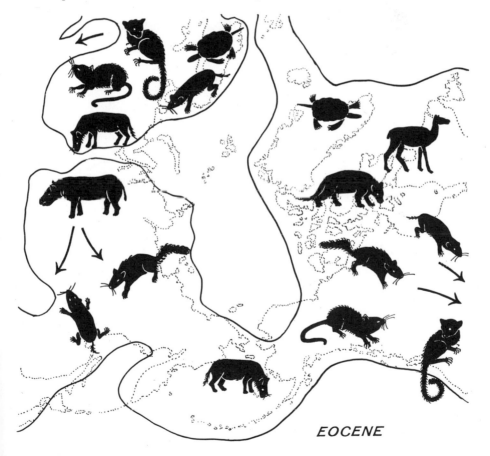

EOCENE

wards, some forty million years, accounts for the horses, hyraxes, jerboas and dormice which the two regions share.

Because the climate is temperate, many typical Old World forms which were once widespread no longer occur in the palearctic, thus differentiating it from the tropical ethiopian and oriental regions. Elephants, rhinoceroses and monkeys, which once ranged over the area, became extinct in the north during the ice ages of the last million years.

Only one family of mammals found in the palearctic has an anomalous distribution, the camel family. The camel family occurs here and in the neotropical but not in the nearctic which lies between. The explanation for this discontinuity lies in the past. The camel family originated in the nearctic in eocene days, sixty million years ago (fig 5.9), spread to the palearctic and neotropical in the pliocene, fifty million years later, when there were continental highways available and then, for some reason, died out in its country of origin, leaving camels in the palearctic and guanacos and their relatives in the neotropical.

THE ACHIEVEMENT OF THE MAPS

On the maps, of the twenty eight land mammal families inhabiting the palearctic, twelve of them are represented, forty three per cent, a smaller total than for the New World regions.

Neither of the two unique families is represented but one of the four shared with the nearctic (the beaver family), one of the four shared ethiopian families (the horses) and the only shared neotropical family (the camels), all occur on the maps. Of the remaining nine families, the most obvious and abundant occur most frequently on the maps: the deer, the bears, the goats and foxes.

Less startling than the New World because, perhaps, taken for granted, the palearctic maps, nevertheless, show nearly half the typical mammalian fauna of the region.

VI

Oriental Region

The oriental region is a comparatively small land area occupying southern Asia. Its southern and western boundaries are clearly defined by the Indian Ocean, its most easterly by the Pacific. It is bounded by the Himalayas in the north from where the foothills run to the Arabian Sea in the west and to the East China Sea in the far east. It includes the Malay peninsula, the Philippines and the large islands of Borneo, Sumatra and Java. Its south-eastern boundary lies among the islands of the Malay Archipelago, where it meets the north-westerly edge of the australian region.

THE FAUNA

Characteristically, the oriental region has an Old World tropical fauna, resembling the ethiopian region in its tropical elements and the palearctic region in its more temperate elements. Thus, its fauna is characterised by the elephants, rhinoceroses, Old World monkeys, lorises, pangolins, chameleons and hornbills which it shares with Africa and by the pheasants which it shares mainly with the palearctic. With its wide variety of reptiles, greater than in any other region, it has an abundance of deer, absent from Africa, parrots and bovids.

Only four mammal families are confined to the area and, of these, two are primates, the tupaiid tree shrews and the tarsiers. The colugo, or so-called flying lemur, forms a third family and the spiny dormice the fourth.

Among the reptiles the gavials, slender nosed fish eating crocodiles, are found nowhere else.

In addition to the unique families and a mixture of Old World tropical and temperate families there are many representatives of widespread families such as bears, cats, squirrels, rats, pigs, snakes, lizards and tree frogs. And the oriental region shares one mammalian family, the tapirs, with the far away neotropical region.

Discontinuously distributed, the tapirs are represented by three species: two in the neotropical region and one in Malaya. The oriental tapir, although resembling the neotropical forms so closely that it is united with them under the same generic name, is strikingly different in its vivid black and white body colour. Once, tapirs occupied the northern lands, presumably covering a wide area from Malaya to Europe and to the New World (Radinsky 1965) but, with the advent of the cold northern conditions of the pleistocene ice ages, they died out from the north, maintaining colonies only in the neotropical and oriental regions.

EARLY RECORDS OF THE FAUNA

A considerable amount of the fauna of the oriental region had been known since the earliest times, when traders visited India from the west.

Marco Polo described the fauna of south-west India at the end of the thirteenth century. 'There are in this country many and divers beasts quite different from those of other parts of the world. Thus there are lions black all over [black leopards or panthers], with no mixture of any other colour; and there are parrots of many sorts, for some are white as snow with red beak and feet, and some are red and some blue, forming the most charming sight in the world; there are green ones too. There are also some parrots of exceeding small size [parakeets], beautiful creatures. They have also very beautiful peacocks, larger than ours and different; and they have cocks and hens quite different from ours and what more shall I say? In short, everything they have is different from ours, and finer and better. Neither is their fruit like ours, nor their beasts, nor their birds, and this difference all comes of the excessive heat. . . . There are also gatpauls [monkeys] in wonderful diversity, with bears, lions, leopards in abundance' (Yule & Cordier 1903). In addition, Marco Polo described elephants and rhinoceroses from the Malayan islands.

Marco Polo stressed the differences between the oriental and the palearctic regions. Others had noticed similarities between the oriental and ethiopian regions. Herodotus had reported that elephants and crocodiles were shared by these two regions and, to these, Strabo had added monkeys, tigers and antdogs. Pliny described chameleons coming from the two regions.

The cartographers have not lavished animals on their oriental regions to the same extent as the other regions: on the T-O maps, the oriental region of the Hereford (fig 2.3), Ebstorf (fig. 9.1) and Vercelli maps contains birds, elephants, a crocodile, unicorn, rhinoceros, yale, a large bovid, lizards, snakes and a parrot; animal inhabitants based on a meagre interpretation of the older naturalists. The maps based on Marco Polo's discoveries show even less interest in the oriental fauna. There are no animals on Fra Mauro's map of the world in 1459 (Bagrow 1964) and the Catalan atlases of the late fourteenth and early fifteenth centuries are mainly concerned with camel, horse or elephant caravans to China or Africa.

In spite of the increasing knowledge of the fauna of the oriental region, it did not seem to attract the cartographers in the same way that other regions had done. By far the most popular representative animals of the oriental region continued to be elephants. This is, perhaps, hardly surprising, since they were well known both as wild animals and, more particularly, as beasts of burden. One of the most spectacular of modern mammals, occurring in only the ethiopian and oriental regions, the elephant represents both these regions abundantly, through the centuries. All early travellers reported large numbers of elephants wherever they touched on the shores of India and Ceylon.

ELEPHANTS

For the most part, very little effort was made to differentiate between the smaller tusked and smaller eared Indian elephant *Elephas* and the altogether larger African elephant *Loxodonta*. Maggiolo drew different elephants in the ethiopian and oriental regions of a 1516 world map which is in the Huntington Library of San Marino, California. Although, on the map, the Indian elephant is larger than the African, their general outlines give a good impression of the difference in shape of the two genera. Furthermore, the ears of the African elephant are fluted and relatively larger than those of the Indian which have a smoother outline. African elephants do, sometimes, frill out their ears when approached and the fluted ears are familiar on early wood cuts of what are mainly African elephants, that of Crescenzi about 1360, for example. Desceliers made a distinction between the two, on both his 1546 and 1550 maps of the world: on both, the African elephants are shown with larger ears than most of those in the Indian region. And, during the century, a map of Ortelius, *Carta dell' Asia* (Almagià 1948), represents the African elephant as generally bigger and taller than the elephant that depicts the oriental region. For the rest, no distinction was made between the two genera and both were shown, frequently, as domesticated animals; though it seems that the Indian elephant was the more usually domesticated of the two, the African elephant having the unjustified reputation of bad temper and waywardness.

That the mapmakers rarely recognised the difference between *Loxodonta* and *Elephas* is hardly surprising when the writings of the naturalists are considered. Strabo maintained that the two were different but mistakenly chose the Indian elephant for the bigger, suggesting that, because the rivers and rains of India were more nourishing than those of Africa, all the animals of India were larger than those of Africa or European Mediterranean lands: 'Ethiopia produces elephants that rival those of India.' Pliny agreed that the Indian elephant was the bigger: 'Elephants are produced by Africa beyond the deserts of Sidra and by the country of the Moors; also by the land of Ethiopia and the cave-dwellers, as has been said, but the biggest ones by India.' Solinus added: 'There are two kinds of them; the nobler sort are known by their greatness, the lesser sort are called bastards.'

Cosmos, writing about AD 545, understood clearly the difference between the two genera: 'The Indian elephants are not furnished with great tusks. . . . The Ethiopians do not understand the art of taming elephants . . . and they are of the kind that have great tusks' (Yule & Cordier 1915). Yet, as late as 1658, in *The History of Four-footed Beasts, Serpents and Insects*, Topsell wrote that it had been said, that the African elephant was greater than the Indian but that he himself did not believe it. It was not until 1799, that Cuvier finally set the two genera apart.

Camels and lions were the next most popular animals of the cartographers: the camels, being mainly domestic, single humped, artificial representatives of the region; the lions, tending towards the heraldic, in many cases. Although not generally associated with India, lions do occur there. But the seemingly more typical tiger is not depicted, although on at least two occasions a distinctive cheetah is found (Le Testu 1555 and van Keulen 1660).

RHINOCEROSES

Fourth in popularity, as faunally characteristic of the region, are the rhinoceroses. Like the elephants, the rhinos are, today restricted in their range to the ethiopian and oriental zoogeographical regions and, only rarely, do they stray on the maps. Unlike the two genera of elephants, the rhinoceroses can be divided into four, two to each region (Simpson 1945).

In Africa, both rhinoceroses, the black rhino *Diceros* and *Ceratotherium* the so-called white rhino (Dutch *weit*, wide; referring to the mouth), have two nasal horns. In the oriental region, the hairy eared Sumatran rhinoceros *Dicerorhinus* has two horns, the distal one being long and the proximal one a small knob; but the great Indian rhinoceros *Rhinoceros* is single horned.

Rhinoceroses had been reported, from both India and Africa, since the early days of faunal records. Aristotle referred to a single horned animal from India and Strabo reported a rhinoceros from Africa.

If Pliny is to be believed, it was Indian rhinoceroses that were brought to Rome for the games. 'At the same games there was also a rhinoceros with one horn on the nose such as has often been seen.' The truth of Pliny's observation is supported by Solinus, who comments that the Romans had not seen an African rhinoceros.

The early mapmakers seem to have relied mainly on Aristotle, portraying the rhinoceros with a single long nasal or forehead horn and the light build of an 'Indian ass' (fig 2.3).

By the end of the thirteenth century, Marco Polo had reported: 'They have hair like that of a buffalo, feet like those of an elephant, and a horn in the middle of the forehead, which is black and very thick. They do no mischief, however, with the horn, but with the tongue alone, for this is covered all over with long and strong prickles. The head resembles that of a wild boar, and they carry it ever bent towards the ground. . . .' In 1516 (Kammerer 1935) and again in 1519, the Homem-Reinel maps figured a good one horned Indian rhinoceros in Bengal conforming to Marco Polo's description except that the horn was drawn more correctly near the tip of the

I

Fig 6.1 From the Homem-Reinel Miller Atlas 1519 in the Bibliothèque Nationale, Paris: lion, one horned rhinoceros, elephants and birds in the oriental region

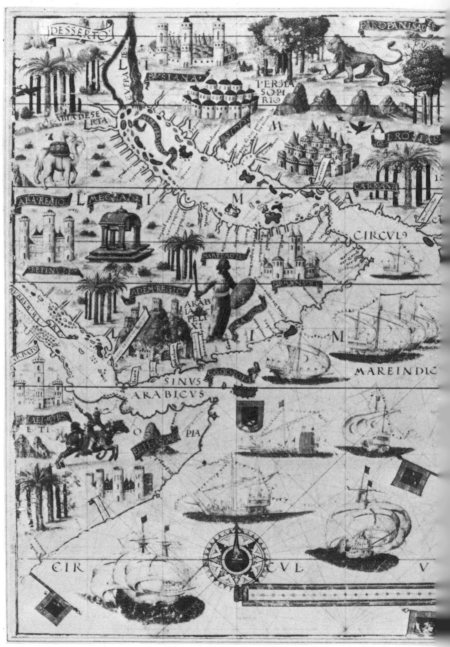

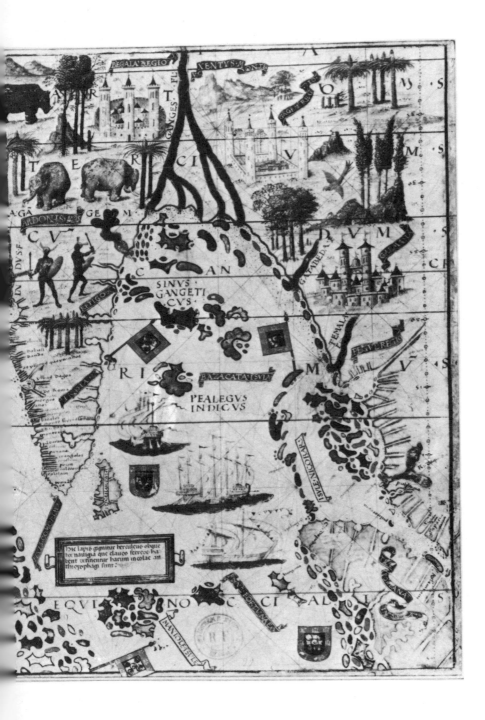

snout (fig 6.1).

By the end of the century, what was to become the standard rhinoceros for years had crept on to the maps: a heavily armour plated Indian rhinoceros with, in addition to its nasal horn, a small forward pointing horn on its shoulders.

This copy of the famous Dürer woodcut of 1515, which had been incorporated as an illustration in Gesner's *Historiae Animalium* in 1551, became standard in the oriental region, in spite of the fact that many of the maps themselves had been constructed from the descriptions of Enciso, who had also described the fauna of the countries extensively in his *Suma de Geographia* 1518, giving an accurate account of an Indian rhinoceros: 'and ther be bestes called Rhynocerotes which be as elephants and almost of their colour, thei be as bygg as a bull and is of making like a hogge saving he hathe his nose croked like a horn and is very hard, wherewith he fighteth with other beastes' (Taylor 1931).

Almost a Dürer rhinoceros occupies southern China in Lin-

Fig 6.2 South China from Linschoten's *Itinerario* 1595: rhinoceros, elephant and possible giraffes

schoten's map of south-east Asia in *Itinerario* 1595 (fig 6.2). Three years later, the rhinoceros has lost the forwardly directed shoulder horn, a small backwardly directed spine of armour being all that remains of this anomaly but, meanwhile, it has become less carefully drawn (fig 6.3). Description, again, was better than draughtsmanship. Linschoten himself had described the animal in 1583. 'They are lesse and lower than the Elephant. It hath a short horne upon the nose, in the hinder part somewhat bigge, and toward the end sharper, of a browne blewe, and whitish colour; it hath a snout like a Hog, and the skin of the upper part of his body is all wrinkled, as if it were armed with shields or Targets' (Purchas 1625).

However, a moderately well drawn Dürer rhinoceros dominates again for the seventeenth century, occurring in the oriental region of several of Blaeu's and de Wit's maps: de Wit's world map of 1660, for example (Wieder 1925).

The representation of what appears to be the hairy eared rhinoceros of the far east in Aldrovandi's *De Quadrupedibus Solidipedibus* of 1616 never appears on maps of the oriental region.

ANTEATING MAMMALS

The 1546 map of Desceliers is particularly interesting in its oriental region, as it depicts what is almost certainly a pangolin, for the first and only time in this region (Jomard 1854). Pangolins are the scaly

Fig 6.3 Rhinoceros from 1598 edition of Linschoten's *Itinerario*

anteaters of the oriental and ethiopian regions, looking like fir cones on legs, with strong digging claws, long snouts, long tongues and prehensile tails.

Desceliers also figures another animal with an elongated snout, which is suspiciously representative of another anteating animal, the antlions, perhaps, of the early naturalists. They had reported the existence of at least two sorts of anteaters and left drawings of dog-like animals and ant-like animals (Druce 1923, James 1929). Vincent de Beauvais described formicaleone as small and mirmicoleon as bigger and, on the Ebstorf map of the thirteenth century, two ant-eating animals had been designated: mirmicaleon in the ethiopian region (fig 2.3) and formica canu, marginally, in the oriental region (fig 9.1). Little can be gained from the actual drawings of these two except that they are different from one another and mirmicaleon is bigger than formica canu.

The pictures on Desceliers' map are easier to interpret, at least in the sense that there is little doubt about the pangolin. The second anteater is more difficult to identify because travellers' reports of the oriental region had not advanced as rapidly as the maps.

Enciso in 1518 is still reporting in much the same language as his predecessors. 'And here be the formicas called *aurifodines* the which in wynter make holes in the grounde wherein thei lie, and the erthe that thei cast out lieth at the mouth of the hole, and among the erthe comes out moche golde and fyne, and therbe none that dare seke thes golde for those aurifodines be perillous beastes and kylle men. . . . Thes formicas be a certeine kynd of lions bigger than a grete foxe, almost as bigge as a wolf, thei be of the same kynde in the ethiope by the equinoctiall' (Taylor 1931). It can be said of this description that it does not fit the pangolin but refers to some carnivore and bears some resemblance to Desceliers' second anteater.

Two anteating carnivores inhabit the oriental region, the sloth-bear *Mellursus* and the ratel or honey badger *Mellivora*.

The sloth-bears have elongated noses and reduced dentition associated with an insect eating diet and huge feet and enormous claws for digging out termites' nests. But the sloth-bear is confined to the oriental region and does not, therefore, fit the written descriptions, although it might be the animal represented by Desceliers.

Ratels live as much on the nests of wasps as termites and ants but they inhabit both the ethiopian and oriental regions. They are badger size, smaller than the sloth-bears, but they have equally huge claws, efficient digging habits, longish snouts and shaggy grey, black and white fur. They are, therefore, 'of the colour of cats' according to Pliny and 'of dogs they have all the form and are just of their size' according to Guillaume Le Clerc in the thirteenth century (Druce 1936). The ratel, too, bears some resemblance to von Cube's description of formica maiones in *Ortus Sanitatus* in 1491. He describes it as occurring in India and Ethiopia, like a wolf with four legs and claws on its feet and figures an extraordinary beast, with a curiously short snout in marked contrast to the characteristically long snout of most ant and termite eating animals. It bears some resemblance to formica canu of the Ebstorf map. Both have pronounced claws and the exceptionally aggressive look of the ratel. Formica canu has a longish snout. Ratels are very aggressive animals, some of the few animals that stand and fight. They dig with great speed into the nests of wasps and bees. The outpouring honey could account for the stories of gold. Jean Fonteneau in 1544 describes them burrowing: 'et icy sont les fourmis appellées arifodunes, lesquelz font fousses dessoutz la terre en lesquelles ilz habitent' (Musset 1904). Their burrowing habits could account for the association with sand (on the Ebstorf map, for example) and sand as much as honey might be the source of the story about gold pouring out of their holes.

The ratel, therefore, is probably one of the anteaters written about and figured on the maps, probably the one on Desceliers' map. A pangolin figures definitely on that map. The two, between them, may well account for the oriental anteaters.

ORIENTAL BIRDS

In 1546, too, Desceliers figures a small bear and, also, a large bird with a crest, which occurs again much later, in 1618, on a map of W. J. Blaeu, for instance.

This bird may represent one of the crested egrets or herons that were common in the region and hunted for their plumes or it might be a sarus crane *Grus antigone* which, though without plumes on its head, is a five foot tall bird, grey, with red legs and head. The sarus crane is specifically figured in several twelfth and thirteenth century bestiaries. These cranes are common features of the south Asia landscape and associated with many legends; never killed by the local people for fear of bad luck, frequently tamed. Cranes, in fact, reach

Fig 6.4 Jungle fowl,
elephant, four horned sheep
and wild boar in the
oriental region of Gutiérrez
world map 1551 in the
Österreichische
Nationalbibliothek, Vienna

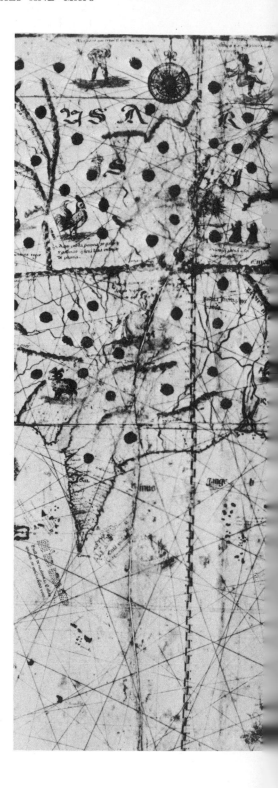

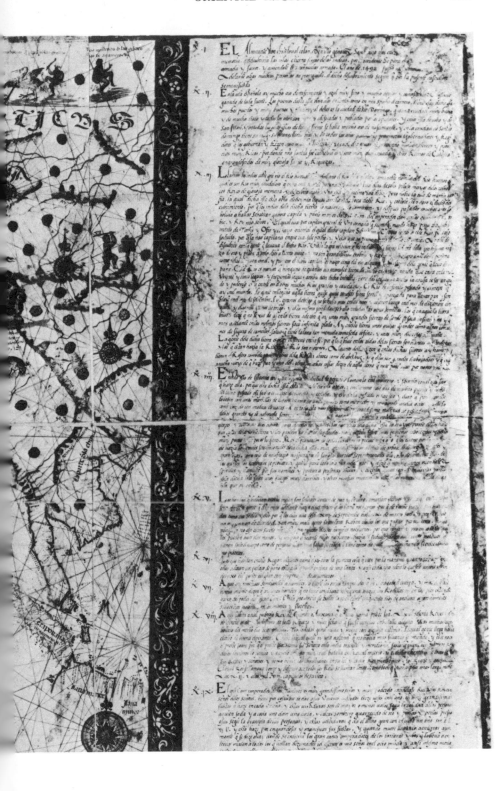

their greatest diversity in Eurasia, being represented both by a large number of species as well as by large numbers of individuals, so that it seems possible that this bird is intended to represent a crane. It is partly red and, on the map, it is a red bird. Egrets are common birds in many other parts of the world and, therefore, seem unlikely to have been picked out specially for the oriental region. The alternative interpretation would be a peacock *Pavo cristatus*. Peacocks had been known from India and associated with the oriental region from earliest times. 'The king of Egypt was presented with a Peacock from India, the largest and most magnificent of its kind,' suggesting that Aelian considered it a particularly oriental bird, an assumption that persisted until 1937, when a peacock was discovered in the Congo (Gilliard 1953). The absence of the spectacular train of the male peacock, on the maps, could be because only the male possesses it and, then, only in the breeding season, while both sexes are crested all the year round. It is interesting that, in the thirteenth century *De Arte Venandi cum Avibus* of Frederick II (Wood & Fyfe 1943), of all the birds figured, only the peacock has a crest and its crest is like a crown like the crests on the maps. In the early bestiaries only the peacock, heron, hoopoe and sometimes the phoenix are crested.

Apart from these animals, the only noteworthy portrayals on the maps are jungle fowl, of which a fine example appears on Gutiérrez' 1551 world map (fig 6.4); a number of pheasants, typical oriental birds; a bird on the Ulpius globe 1542 (fig 6.6), which bears a close resemblance to the black ibis *Pseudibis papillosa* of Gesner 1551; and the hornbill that flies over the Old World of Le Testu's 1566 map of the world in company with pheasant and bird of paradise (fig 9.3).

OMISSIONS

The monkeys, langurs and apes are, surprisingly, not represented, although many would consider them outstanding members of the fauna.

Less surprising is the absence of the black and white Malay tapir whose New World counterpart eventually reached maps of South America. The oriental tapir is a rare animal and is confined to the deep forests of Burma, Malaya and Sumatra where its bold contrasting pattern, though striking in captivity, would tend to make it nearly invisible. It was not discovered and brought out of the forest alive until 1805 and the first written description appeared in 1816 (Raffles 1821).

None of the unique oriental families occur on maps: tree shrews, tarsiers, flying lemurs, spiny dormice or gavial crocodiles, for instance.

But omissions are, as usual, greater than errors.

UNICORNS

The most constant error of the oriental region is the unicorn (fig 6.5). Interestingly, in those drawings whose details can be observed, the unicorn is, distinctly, a cloven hoofed animal, not the single hoofed horse that it eventually became in English heraldry. It is unlikely that the unicorn is a confusion of early reporters' tales of rhinoceroses because, from early times, a distinction was made between the rhinoceros with a horn on its nose and the monoceros which, according to Pliny, had cloven hoofs and was an antelope. He added that, unlike many horned animals, the female unicorn was also horned. Solinus gave it the body of a horse. Isidore of Seville (Megenburg 1481) described the unicorn as a small animal, a description hardly applicable to most rhinoceroses; further, he made a distinction between the rhinoceros and the monoceros, as all previous writers had done.

It seems clear that the unicorn was one of the straight horned, cloven hoofed ungulates. Cloven hoofed ungulates lie down typically by first bending the forelegs to a kneeling position, thus conforming to the pictures of the unicorn kneeling to put its head in the lap of a virgin. Horse-like ungulates, including the rhinoceroses, first bend the hind legs, into a sitting position, before lying.

The most obviously straight horned of the Asian cloven hoofed ungulates are the horse-antelopes, the gazelles and the goat-gazelles. The horse-antelopes have very long horns and, as their name implies, a heavier more horse-like build and tail than most other antelopes, thus conforming to the descriptions of both Pliny and Solinus. The oryx and the addax are horse-antelopes.

According to Aldrovandi, in 1612, the unicorn is called oryx although, in a detailed and accurate description of the oryx in 212, Oppian had clearly written of two horns (Mair 1958).

Seen in profile, however, an oryx might easily be thought to have only one horn; or an oryx might lose a horn and become a unicorn (Cuvier 1817, Shepard 1930).

From earlier civilisations, many examples can be found of horned animals represented with only one horn. Sometimes, this was paralleled by the depiction of only one fore leg and one hind leg, as in the

Aurignacian drawings, of approximately thirty thousand years ago, at Pairnon-Pair in France and those of the Bovidians of the Sahara, of some six thousand years ago (Lhote 1959). At other times, there were four legs but only one horn, as on Greek vases and as may be seen in the reproduction on modern Greek match boxes. The weak point in this argument, from the point of view of the oriental region, is that the ideal unicorn, the oryx, is primarily an African animal (with one species occurring in Arabia and, perhaps until recently, more northerly deserts) although it is known that both the addax and oryx were domesticated by the Egyptians (Zeuner 1963) and might, therefore, have been taken from Africa to India or China. Unicorns are often described in captivity: by Lewes Vertomanus in 1503 (Eden 1555), for example.

Failing the oryx, there is a wide variety of gazelles and goat-gazelles *Procapra* that range over Eurasia and could provide unicorn prototypes. *Pantholops hodgsonii* the chiru of Tibet is a rare straight horned goat to which many legends have become attached. Timotheos mentions an oryx of the Hydaspes which has been identified as the chiru by Keller (1909). Blundeville 1594, not the most reliable

Fig 6.5 Unicorns in India from Linschoten's *Itinerario* 1596

of naturalists, maintained that there were at least two sorts of unicorn, one of which inhabited Africa and the other India. The African form had cloven feet, a mane and a long horn, the Indian form was called the Indian Asse. Thus, the Indian unicorn corresponded to the 'wild asses' of Ktesias: 'as large as horses, some being even larger. Their head is of a dark red colour, their eyes blue, and the rest of their body white. They have a horn in their forehead, a cubit in length' (McCrindle 1882).

Perhaps the confusion, between the rhinoceros and the monoceros, or unicorn, stems from Aristotle's observation that cloven hoofed animals never have a single horn and, for this reason, his reference to the Indian rhinoceros as an Indian ass. Even so, the confusion was not universal because some, like Pliny, continued to distinguish between the unicorn and rhinoceros. Justel 1674 reports an anonymous Portuguese explorer writing: 'It is not to be confused with a rhinoceros because the rhinoceros has two horns a bit arched. The unicorn is as big as a splendid horse of dark bay colour, with maine and tail black and a long whiteish horn. They live in woods and are very timid and not often seen. Others from the plains report a unicorn rather smaller like a genet d'Espagne (barbary horse).'

There is such a wide variety of antelopes and gazelles from which to choose a unicorn that it is difficult to reach a final decision. More than likely there is not one unicorn but at least two, the Afro-Arabian horse-antelope, oryx, and the Asian goat-gazelle, chiru.

SEROWS AND GIRAFFES

On the Ulpius globe, of 1542, in the library of the New York Historical Society, are two interesting ungulates in northern Indo-China (fig 6.6). They have two long backwardly curved horns and long floppy ears. The indische Hausziegen had appeared with short horns, cloven feet and floppy ears, in a travel book by Breydenbach in 1488 and they turn up again, in 1551, in Gesner's *Historiae Animalium*, described as Capris indicus. On the Ulpius globe, their horns are much longer than in either of these other representations. In 1583, Martines figures the short horned variety in his atlas, in the Bibliothèque Nationale in Paris and, in 1655, on Blaeu's far-eastern sheet of his map of the world at the National Maritime Museum, Greenwich, they are figured without the floppy ears.

Fig 6.6 Indo-China from the Ulpius Globe 1542 in the library of the New
York Historical Society: ibis, Indian goats, giraffe and lions

No animal fits the picture adequately. One of the problems is
that the size of both the horns and the ears varies, according to the
author. It is just possible that they represent nothing more exciting
than a particular breed of goats from the oriental region.

They may, however, be one of the wild goats, in which the region
abounds and it is tempting to suggest the serow *Capricornis*, a goat

related to the chamois and having long mule-like ears and curved horns. Serows range over China, Japan, Burma and Malaya wherever there are mountains.

Another curious ungulate, that appears on Gutiérrez' 1551 map of the world, is a four horned sheep (fig 6.4). This may be only an abnormal sheep, of which many examples are known but, less likely, it might be the four horned antelope *Tetracerus quadricornis* of India.

Even more interesting is the occurrence in the oriental region of an animal with a very long neck which is not obviously a camel: the Ulpius globe 1542 (fig 6.6); the Linschoten map 1595 (fig 6.2); the W. J. Blaeu World map of 1618. It bears a close resemblance to a heavy giraffe: the long neck is clearly exaggerated, the animal has two short horns, comparatively large ears, a long face and a long upper lip so typical of giraffes.

Today, the giraffe family, giraffes and okapis, are confined to the ethiopian region but once, less than a million years ago, they roamed over Asia. According to some early writers, Pausanius and Timotheos, the giraffe occurred in India. This supposition was based on somewhat tenuous evidence in some cases: the report, for instance, of Timotheos 'that the giraffe is an Indian animal; and it is born from the intercourse of different animals. That a man dealing in Indian products . . . passed through Gaza bringing two giraffes and an elephant to the Emperor Anastasius' (Bodenheimer & Rabinowitz 1948). In 1658, Topsell was still reporting that giraffes were plentiful in India, as well as Ethiopia, at the time he was writing; but he is not a reliable author. However, Buffon, in 1765, described them from the desert regions of Ethiopia, Arabia and India. Others, quoting Artemidor for instance, reported giraffes in Arabia (Strabo). But the majority, Pliny, Isidore of Seville and Cosmos the Monk, for example, confined the giraffes to Africa. Like the oryx, however, the giraffe was frequently kept in captivity, locally in Africa as well as elsewhere, see p. 00. Frederick II had a giraffe in his menagerie in Europe at the beginning of the thirteenth century and Gonzales de Clavijo described a giraffe with considerable accuracy which he had seen in Azerbaijan in Persia, in 1405, brought from Babylon by merchants (Markham 1859). Perhaps it was these domesticated animals, misplaced because the author saw them in captivity without knowing their country of origin or, with no Aristotelean evidence to fall back on, the practice of calling giraffes camels led to the confusion: 'Indian camels resemble leopards in their colour' (Pausanius); 'Aethiopian camel' (Wotton 1552).

But the case of the giraffe may have other interpretations.

Fossils known from the oriental pleistocene belong to the same genus *Giraffa* as modern African giraffes. The question is, therefore, apparent. Has the extinction of the giraffe in Asia occurred in historic times, its representation on maps being based on the actual experience of someone or, was the extinction prehistoric and the reports and drawing based on legend and hearsay with a firm basis in fact, or is the whole thing the imagination of the cartographers and men like Topsell and the result of carrying the similarities of the ethiopian and oriental regions too far? It is impossible to answer these questions, at present, but when the prehistory of the oriental region becomes better known, if cave paintings are found, an answer may be formulated. So far the evidence, neither direct nor strictly relevant, is that a Sumerian bronze figure shows remarkable resemblance to a related fossil genus of giraffes *Sivatherium* from India (Colbert 1955).

ORIGIN OF THE ORIENTAL FAUNA

Neither cartographically nor actually is the fauna of the oriental region as striking as some of the other regions. Its unique animals are small and obscure both in temperament and zoologically. Its Old World tropical element has not the same variety and eye catching interest of its similar counterpart in Africa and its Old World temperate element would seem of little interest to travellers and, even less, to cartographers.

This situation is a reflection of the history of the oriental region. At the beginning of the cenozoic, when South America and Africa were already isolated continents, the oriental region formed part of the great Asian continent and shared its fauna. This continuity persisted after Africa had regained a connexion with the north in early oligocene or, even earlier, eocene times, so that much of the ethiopian, palearctic and oriental fauna mixed. The Old World had zoological reality. Only during miocene and pliocene days did the great orogenic events occur that led to the building of the new mountains of the world, the Andes, the Alps and the Himalayas. Gradually, the mountain ranges blocked intermigrations. The Himalayas blocked exchanges between north and south. Finally, with the advent of desert conditions in Arabia and Baluchistan, there was again almost no interchange between the oriental and ethiopian regions. The northeastern boundary of the oriental region, with the palearctic, was never so effectively blocked as that between the oriental and the ethiopian. There is still the possibility of slight intermigration along the coastal areas of east China (Wallace 1876).

Of recent identity, the oriental contains a typical sample of Old

K

World tropical animals obtained either from the north, where they have later become extinct in the face of the cold, or from Africa while there was a migration route. In addition, many more typically temperate animals from the north have flourished in the oriental, such as the deer which never invaded the ethiopian region. Owing to its short period of isolation, few unique families are found in the region.

The oriental region of the cartographers, too, is not a rich zoological region but, within its modest limits, it shows some of the animals that the oriental shares with other regions: the elephants, rhinoceroses, a monkey, a pangolin and crocodiles with the ethiopian, for instance; some, like the deer, cranes, pheasants, which are more typically shared with the temperate regions; and others, like the lions, which are of more widespread distribution. An outstanding exception to this is the goat subfamily, the Caprinae, of which almost all the genera inhabit Asia. Omitting the domesticated variety, this subfamily is well represented only in the oriental region of the maps. At least a third of the living Asian forms seem to be represented, in the oriental region and nowhere else, even if some of them do take the somewhat bizarre forms of unicorn, alce mulo and capris indicus. However, only just over a third of the oriental land mammal families are represented on the maps (eleven out of thirty) which is considerably fewer than in the other regions. But, its striking similarity to the ethiopian region is shown by the occurrence of half the shared families. It is curious that some of the most characteristic oriental families, the monkeys and the squirrels, either do not occur or occur only rarely on the maps.

VII

Ethiopian Region

The ethiopian region comprises, with the oriental region, the tropical area of the Old World. In the east, the south and the west, it is clearly defined by the Indian and Atlantic oceans. In the north, the boundary is formed by the Sahara desert and the deserts of Arabia. Thus, in zoogeography, the ethiopian region includes most of Arabia and Egypt and excludes the most northerly part of Africa.

But, continuing the convention adopted in the earlier part, because of the inaccuracy of the early maps, the whole African continent will be discussed as the ethiopian region. In fact, as more of Africa came to be represented on the maps, so the animals receded from the north coastal strip and became, zoogeographically, more accurate.

Some zoogeographers include Madagascar in the ethiopian region, others do not. But it is so rarely populated with animals, by cartographers, that neither its fauna nor its zoogeographical status will be considered.

COMMON MAP ANIMALS

For animals, the ethiopian region is unsurpassed. Its fauna was represented from the earliest days of mapmaking and, although even African maps were denuded of animals by the eighteenth century, elephants occur as late as 1782 on a map by de la Rochette (Tooley 1949) and several other maps, only a few years earlier, were richly populated. A Dutch map, by Brink, the surveyor on the Hop expedition to South Africa in 1761, for instance, has a wildebeeste, zebra, giraffe and horse (Hop 1778, Koeman 1952). Inhabited maps of the ethiopian region run through six centuries.

But the fauna of the Nile had been given permanent pictorial representation in Europe, long before that, in the mosaics preserved in Palestrina, Pompeii and Sicily.

A considerable range of animals inhabits the ethiopian, from the earliest times, but the predominant animals, through the centuries, are the elephants, camels and lions. Ostriches lost their early popularity, to some extent, lying in fourth place after the fifteenth century. Then came monkeys, rhinoceroses, dragons and crocodiles. In fact, there had been little general expansion of the fauna since the early maps, by which time all these animals had occurred on the continent, some of them frequently.

There is little to be said for the advancement in accuracy of drawings either. On some maps, the animals tended to be formalised, Alonso de Santa Cruz 1542 (Nordenskiöld 1889), for example; on others, they settled down to comparatively standard forms.

The elephants, early, acquired their pillar legs and large ears, but there was considerable uncertainty still over the provenance of their tusks, see p. 43. In some of all periods (Homem-Reinel 1519, Desceliers 1550, Prunes' 1586 portolan in the Bibliothèque Nationale, Paris, for instance) the tusks came, erroneously, from the lower jaw while in many no decision was taken. But, by the seventeenth century, the Dutch cartographers were drawing the tusks, consistently, from the upper jaw.

An interesting elephant occurs, in Le Testu's 1555 *Cosmographie Universelle*, with the tusks hanging from the mouth (fig 7.13). It is difficult to decide whether they originate from the upper or lower jaw but, from the way they lie, it seems probable that Le Testu knew that they came from the upper jaw but was uncertain about the orientation. The tusks follow the more usual alignment of long incisors, hanging, from the upper jaw, downwards.

From the sixteenth century, most elephants were figured as wild animals, without the domestic trappings of the earlier ones.

Camels, too, from a domesticated beginning, had a tendency to be depicted as wild animals, later on. Most camels were of the Mediterranean domesticated one humped variety but, occasionally, a two humped form appears. In Maggiolo 1516, Agnese 1543 (Bibliothèque Nationale, Paris) and in Le Testu 1555, two humped camels made their appearance in north Africa.

MORE RHINOCEROSES

Rhinoceroses had been well known members of the African fauna from remotest times. In the Barberini mosaic *L'Inondazione del Nilo* the rhinoceros appears as a pig-like animal with three toes, small tufted ears, a short tail and two short nasal horns, the front one somewhat larger than the back one. This animal is firmly labelled 'rinokemus'. It is a very fair representation of the African black rhinoceros and a great deal better than the slim, maned rhinoceros of the Hereford map which, anyway, having only one long nasal horn, more nearly represents the oriental rhinoceros.

Many of the early writers were aware that the African rhinoceros had two nasal horns. Pausanias wrote: 'I have likewise seen the Aethiopian bull, which they call rhinoceros, because a horn projects from the extremity of its nostril, and another small one under: but it has no horns on its head' (Taylor 1824). Many others, including Cosmos the Monk, wrote of more than one horn on the ethiopian rhinoceros.

Some had even contrasted the ethiopian and oriental rhinoceroses. Timotheos wrote that rhinoceros was the name for the African rhinoceros and that rhinoceroses from India were called oxen. Centuries later, Nicolo de Conti could be more precise. Of the Indian rhinoceros, he wrote, in 1444: 'Also there is a certaine Beast, having a head like unto a Hogge, the tayle lyke unto an oxe, and a horne in his forehead, like unto a unicorne, but smaller by a cubite. He is in coulore and bignesse like unto the Elephante' and, later, of the African rhinoceros, 'also there is a kind of beastes of divers couloures like unto the Elephant, but they have not such a trunk and snoute, they do call him Belus. They have feete like unto a Camell, and two very sharp hornes, each of a cubit in length, the one standeth in his forehead and the other upon his nose' (Penzer 1937). The cartographers were less clear about the differences, though many of them were aware that rhinoceroses inhabited both the ethiopian and oriental regions.

In 1516, rhinoceroses occur, on different maps, in both the oriental and the ethiopian regions but, in each case, they are a one horned variety. The oriental rhino of Homem-Reinel resembled an elephant, except for its terminal horn and lack of a trunk. Waldseemüller's African rhino (fig 7.1), on the other hand, was a heavily armoured three toed single horned beast, with considerable likeness to the

great Indian rhinoceros. It was as good an Indian rhino as the Barberini
mosaic was a good African one. L. Fries copied Waldseemüller's
rhino on his maps of Africa in 1520 and 1524 (Bagrow 1959).

Thereafter, the rhinoceros deteriorated on the maps probably
owing to the influence of Gesner and subsequent naturalists who
had accepted Dürer's rhinoceros as the only rhinoceros. The lack
of realisation that there were several genera of rhinoceroses and the
false lead given by Gesner caused confusion among the naturalists
for many years. Thus, Topsell 1607 declared: 'Euchemis saith, that
the Rhinoceros hath two horns in his nose, but that is utterly false,
as you may see from the picture [Dürer's]: although Martial seems

Fig 7.1 Waldseemüller's African rhinoceros from the *Carta Marina* 1516
in Schloss Wolfegg

to expresse so much in these verses.' But Justel 1674 reports a Portuguese author: that the rhinoceros cannot be confused with the unicorn because the rhinoceros has two horns a bit arched.

Buffon finally dismissed the Dürer rhinoceros but described and figured accurately only the great Indian rhinoceros in 1754 but, in the supplement in 1776, the confusion takes shape once more. Buffon concludes that there are two horned rhinoceroses after all and that they form a variety of the one horned version. Furthermore, he declares that they are found equally in Asia and Africa. At this point it seems to be believed that both one and two horned forms occurred both in Africa and Asia. Certainly, in 1778, an engraving

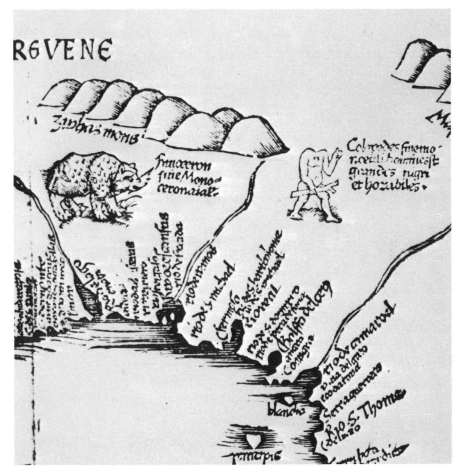

Fig 7.2 Rhinoceros in the Ptolemaeus Argentorata *Geographica* 1525

of what purports to be a south African rhino has only one horn, midway up his nose (Hop 1778).

On the maps confusion was even greater. In the early part of the sixteenth century, following on Waldseemüller and Fries, came the rhinoceros of the 1525 *Ptolemaeus Argentorata* (Nordenskiöld 1897), a debased version of the former, its single horn now large and with a saw edge (fig 7.2). A more pig-like version inhabits the Africa of Peter Apian's world map of 1530 in the British Museum (fig 7.3). By 1542, the Dürer shoulder horned rhinoceros had arrived, on the Ulpius globe. A single horned Indian rhinoceros with cloven feet occurs five years later in the Africa of the Vallard atlas (fig 7.4).

1550 saw two versions of African rhinoceroses: Desceliers' curious saw nosed animal on a map of the world, possibly a further deterioration from the original Waldseemüller, possibly a drawing hesitating between one and two horns (fig 7.5); and an anonymous chart of the Atlantic that decides for one horn and elephant pillar legs (fig 7.6).

Three years later, Desceliers, on another map of the world, destroyed in 1915 (Oberhummer 1924), made another attempt and redrew his rhino (fig 7.7). This time it was a more distinctly three toed animal with a short thin tail in contrast to the bushy tail that had been creeping in and its single nasal horn had the saw edge towards the animal instead of away from it as in earlier versions. In 1555 yet another rhinoceros had occurred, in Le Testu's *Cosmographie Universelle*. This was a tall, scaly animal with three functional toes and a huge curved horn from half way along the nose (fig 7.12). In 1558, in the Homem atlas (Cortesão & Teixeira da Mota 1960), the rhinoceros was well armoured with four clawed toes on each foot and one long curving nasal horn (fig 7.8). After 1558, the Dürer rhinoceros, which had appeared in Africa in 1542 and the oriental region in 1595 (Linschoten), persisted both on the maps and in the works on natural history until, according to Buffon, an Indian rhinoceros was correctly described in 1735.

SIMILARITIES BETWEEN ETHIOPIAN AND ORIENTAL REGIONS

Whatever their inaccuracies in detail, the most frequently recurring animals of the ethiopian region gave a reasonably good picture of

Fig 7.3 Apian's map of the world 1530 in the British Museum, London: rhinoceros in the ethiopian region; birds in the oriental region; macaw in the neotropical region

Fig 7.4 West Africa from the Vallard Atlas 1547 in the Huntington Library, California: cattle, rhinoceros, elephant, camels, monkeys, crocodiles, lions, antelopes (impala or gerenuk), small carnivores and parrot

the Old World tropics. Furthermore, the ethiopian shared on the maps its elephants, lions, camels, rhinoceroses and crocodiles with the oriental region. Thus, some of the outstanding similarities between the regions were given due representation by the cartographers. Monkeys were not often part of the oriental scene although they figured largely in the ethiopian. The camels were, of course, strays from the palearctic, except in their domesticated state.

The ethiopian region shares eight mammalian families with the oriental region alone: elephants, rhinoceroses, chevrotains, lorises, Old World monkeys, apes, bamboo rats and pangolins. The elephants and rhinoceroses are well represented on the maps. Monkeys occur mainly in the ethiopian region of the maps where they are abundant and range through the long tailed monkeys, macaques or guenons (Desceliers 1550) and a naked buttocked drill (Le Testu 1555), to a lion maned baboon on a late sixteenth century Italian portolan of the Mediterranean (Winter 1950). The loris and ape families would not be expected to be distinguishable from the monkeys of these early dates. Of the other shared families, chevrotains and bamboo rats do not appear and the pangolin is an occasional visitor to both regions in Wells' *New Sett of Maps* 1701, for example (fig 7.9 and see p.159).

Crocodiles and dragons occur in both regions but chameleons, which are shared by the two with their main centre of diversification in Africa, occur mainly on maps of the ethiopian region. According to Pliny: 'Africa also has the chameleon, although India produces it in greater numbers. . . . And it is more remarkable for the nature of its colouring, since it constantly changes the hue of its eyes and tail and whole body and always makes it the colour with which it is in closest contact, except red and white.'

DRAGONS

Dragons and flying snakes are frequent. These are animals that are normally labelled mythical and dismissed. Certainly, some of the drawings are highly speculative but some, nevertheless, are no worse impressionistic representations of real animals than some of the rhinoceroses and some of the South American mammals. Several genera of snakes are known as flying snakes, *Chlorophis* the African colubrid

Fig 7.5 From Desceliers' 1550 map of the world in the British Museum, London: camels, cattle, horses, rhinoceroses, dragons, carnivore and snakes

green tree snakes, for example. They do not have wings but they shoot from trees, holding themselves rigid by curving the scales and muscles of the ventral part of the body. By progressing through the air, they merit the name flying snakes. Although coiled, Desceliers' 1550 flying snake is propelled through the air and without wings (fig 7.5). Le Testu's 1555 flying snakes are both with and without wings (fig 7.13). In addition to the flying snakes, numerous more ordinary forms occur on the maps.

The frequently occurring dragons are even less fanciful, at least for the oriental region. Small lizards, belonging to the genus *Draco*, have membranes stretched over elongated ribs to provide brilliantly coloured parachute wings, with which they can glide from trees. Of the many species, some have monstrous formations of the head. Pomponius Mela described the flying serpents of Arabia about AD 43: 'Of serpents the worthiest to be had in remembrance, are those which

Fig 7.6 Rhinoceros and lion in the west Africa of an anonymous chart of the Atlantic in the Bodleian Library, Oxford

being very little (and whose stinging is present death) are reported to come forth of the frozen Fennes at certain times of the yeare, and from thence flying in flockes towards Aegipe' (Golding 1590). And Pausanias wrote: 'I have never indeed seen winged serpents, but I am persuaded there are such animals' and the picture of 'le serpent ailé' of Belon 1557 bears considerable resemblance to *Draco* except that it has only two legs, a mistake perpetuated for many centuries.

> Dangereuse est du serpent la nature,
> Qu'on voit voler pres de mont Sinai
> Qui me serait, de le voir, esbahy,
> Si on a peur, voyant sa portraiture.

The range of the genus is across the whole of southern Asia and Arabia so that, although they do technically just come to the ethiopian region, they are not strictly continental African animals. When they occur on African maps, they are sometimes scattered across the continent but, frequently, they are confined to the more north-easterly areas which, often, include Arabia. The cartographers had varied opinions on the structure of *Draco* for sometimes it has two legs and sometimes four, the two legged variety being just in the

Fig 7.7 Rhinoceros from Desceliers' map of the world 1553

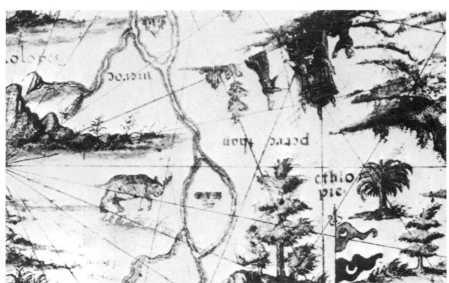

Fig 7.8 Rhinoceros from the Homem Atlas of 1558 in the British Museum, London

majority. Apart from the Ebstorf and Gutiérrez 1551 dragons, which show some resemblance to the one most commonly found in bestiaries, the cartographers seem not to have been influenced by the books of animal drawings, nor very markedly by one another. The best *Draco* occurs on a 1683 map of Abyssinia by Ludolfi in Allardt's *Atlas Major* (fig 7.10). This one has four legs, wing membranes supported from the thorax and a typical *Draco* head, resembling very closely *D. volans* of Malaya with orange and black wings (Gadow 1901), a picture much superior to the two legged variety of Gesner, Belon and Topsell as late as 1658.

AFFINITIES WITH THE NORTH

Mixed with this mainly tropical fauna are a few palearctic animals: dormice, jerboas, conies and wild horses, as well as the hyenas and Old World porcupines, which the ethiopian shares with both

Fig 7.9 Nubia from Wells *A New Sett of Maps* 1701

the palearctic and the oriental. Both the horses and hyenas are represented on the maps, horses as domestic horses, wild horses and, in a few cases, zebras: Speed's *Prospect* 1626 (fig 7.11) and several subsequent Mercator-Hondius *Atlas* maps. 'Here is also the zevera or zebra,' according to Andrew Battell writing between 1589 and 1607, 'which is like an horse, but that his mane, his taile, his strokes of divers colours downe his sides and legges, doe make a difference. These zeveras are all wilde, and live in great herds, and will suffer a man to come within shot of them, and let them shoote three or four times at them before they will run away' (Purchas 1625).

A porcupine is probably represented on the 1655 Blaeu world map at Greenwich, the 1659 Blaeu map of Africa in the *Klencke Atlas* about 1660 in the British Museum and the Coronelli atlas 1691–1696 in Paris. It had been reported from Africa by Solinus as being 'very ryfe in those Countries a beast like a Hedghog, wyth a hyde full of rough brystles, which he oftentimes looseneth of his owne accorde, and darteth them foorth so thicke as it were a showre of pricks' (Golding 1590). An African porcupine had been figured by Gesner in 1551 and many visitors reported either the porcupines themselves or quantities of porcupine quills.

In addition, the maps portray leopards, unicorns, cattle and antelopes, animals of a reasonably wide distribution. The unicorns, already discussed, may be the horse-antelope oryx or addax or a con-

L

fusion with the rhinoceros. 'We enquired above in the country if they had any knowledge of the Unicorne, and they have told me that higher within the Land is a beast which hath one horne only in his fore-head, but describe him as to be of the colour and bignesse of a fallow Deer, and the horne to be about the length of their arme, and no otherwise; not like that which we have described of which I doubt whether there be any such,' wrote Richard Jolson in 1620 (Purchas 1625). And, 150 years later, in 1773, Michael Collinson wrote to the American botanist John Bartram: 'With regard to the unicorn I am rather divided in my judgment, even in respect to their present existence, in the interior region of Africa, of which, at this period, we are extremely ignorant' (Darlington 1849).

Some of the cattle on the maps seem to represent the native eland with its humped back (Oliva's atlas 1625 in the Bibliothèque Nationale, Paris; Janssonius' *Novus Atlas* 1646; Blaeu's world map 1648), although it is difficult to decide whether the drawings are meant to represent wild bovids or domestic cattle. Other cloven hoofed animals occur frequently but not as frequently as might be expected, considering the spectacular radiation of the antelope subfamily in Africa. Small horned dorcas gazelle *Gazella* appear on the 1504 Maggiolo world map and on some of the Hondius and Blaeu maps of the mid-seventeenth century (fig 7.11). Some of the bigger antelopes, too, are figured such as impala *Aepyceros* on the Oliva portolan of the Mediterranean in the library of the Hispanic Society of America in New York and in the Vallard atlas 1547 (fig 7.4). The impala

Fig 7.10 From a map of Abyssinia by Ludolfi 1683 in Allardt's *Atlas Major*: single horned rhinoceros but typically African elephants with large ears and a flying lizard *Draco volans*

had been referred to by name in an account of a journey in Angola by Eduardo Lopes in 1588 (Purchas 1625) and gazelles were frequently named by travellers. Erroneously, they also wrote of stags and deer and, from time to time, branched horned deer do appear on maps of Africa.

The ethiopian region is essentially Old World in its mammalian fauna. It has no families which it shares only with either the nearctic or the neotropical. Some of its reptiles, amphibia and fish are similar to those of the neotropical but this likeness extends only doubtfully to the birds and not at all to the mammals, unless some rodent families of Africa are confirmed to have affinities with neotropical forms. There are, of course, members of all classes in Africa that are of world wide occurrence.

ENDEMIC FAMILIES

Competing in number with the tropics of the New World, the ethiopian region has twelve unique families of mammals, several birds including ostriches and secretary birds, a lizard and turtle family as well as an amphibian and several fish families.

Three of the endemic mammal families are little known insectivores: golden moles, elephant-shrews and African water shrews. A further six unique families are rodents, difficult to distinguish from the better known northern rodents. The remaining three unique families are large distinctive animals: the giraffes, hippopotamuses and the aardvark.

Giraffes occur accurately drawn on early mosaics of the African fauna (fig 2.9), go through the nearly unrecognisable camelopardalis of the thirteenth century Ebstorf map (fig 2.2), through the formalised long necked animal of the Genoese world map of 1457 (fig 2.8), to the excellently drawn slender animal of Nicolo de Caveri in 1502, influenced possibly by one of the early woodcuts such as Breydenbach 1488. 'Also', wrote Nicolo de Conti in 1444, 'they reported that there is another kind of Beast, of nine cubits in length, and sixe foot in height, having cloven feete like unto an Oxe. Their body is a cubit in compasse, and much like in haire unto the Libard, headed like unto a Camell, and hathe a necke of four cubits in length. His tayle is very thicke, and much esteemed, for the women do worke with it, embroidering it with precious stones, hanging them at their armes' (Penzer 1937). The giraffe degenerates to a camelopardalis in 1504 on

Fig 7.11 A Hondius map of north Africa from Speed's *Prospect of the Most Famous Parts of the World* 1631: camel, lions, gazelle, dragon, crocodile, monkeys, ostriches, zebra and elephants

Maggiolo's map and on Ribeiro's map of 1529 (fig 10.1); but returns as an elegant Gesner giraffe, on the Prunes maps of 1559 in the Library of Congress and 1586 in the Bibliothèque Nationale, Paris. Another version, with comparatively long horns, makes its appearance on Coronelli globes and in atlases and then puts in a final realistic appearance in 1761, on the Dutch map of the coast of South Africa by Brink (Koeman 1952). On the whole, these African giraffes are more realistic than those that occur so suspiciously in the oriental region.

Although not as frequently a symbol of Africa as the elephants, camels and lions, the giraffe occurs, regularly, through the centuries from the thirteenth to the eighteenth. On at least four occasions, the giraffe had strayed to Asia and, in 1566, the Le Testu world map, about which more will be said later, depicts an unmistakable giraffe in the palearctic region (fig 9.3). Giraffes occur in both North and South America in the Pasterot Livre de la Marine 1587 and giraffes, or they may be llamas, occur in Coronelli's South America of globes 1688–1696 and the Atlante Veneto 1691–1696.

The other two unique mammal families of large distinctive animals are rare on the maps.

Surprisingly, the hippo which was always described in detail by the early travellers makes few appearances. Hippos occur on the Ulpius globe 1542 in somewhat strange form (fig 7.12); and on a map of Abyssinia by F. Eschinardus in 1684 (Youssouf Kamal 1926–51). 'They live,' according to Duarte Pacheco Pereira 1505–1508, 'in the river, usually in the shallow parts with the water up to their belly, but also in the depths when they choose; they also come ashore to graze and lie in the sun' (Kimble 1937). Hippos feature as an inset to a map of Africa by G. Valk in 1680 and, probably, in the Coronelli atlas of 1691–1696.

Less surprising is the absence, from most maps, of the aardvark or Cape anteater Orycteropus. In 1529, Ribeiro features a mixed population of animals in Africa, one of which might represent an aardvark (fig 10.1). It has long ears, claws and, although otherwise not unlike a hyena, is distinguishable from the more obvious hyena and jackal on the map by the thin tail, contrasting with the bushy tails of the carnivores. 'They live upon Ants,' wrote Friar Joanno dos Sanctos when he visited east Africa, 'putting their tongues (two spans and a half long, like a wax candle) into the Ant-holes (which they scrape with their claws) whereon the Ants running they pull it in and so

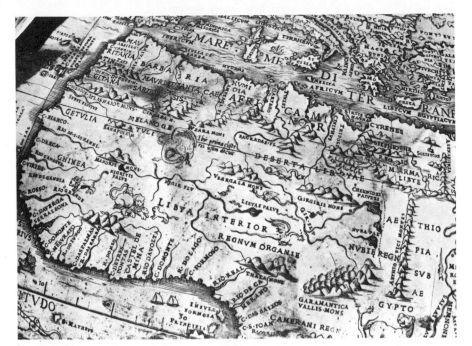

Fig 7.12 Part of Africa from the Ulpius Globe 1542 in the library of the New York Historical Society: pelican, snakes, dragons, lions and hippopotamus

feed and fill themselves. . . . The snout is very long and slender, long eares like a Mule, without haire, the taile thick and strait of a spanne long, fashioned at the end lyke a Distaffe' (Purchas 1625). This excellent description was written in 1597. Le Testu's map of south Africa, in 1555, shows an animal that has several characteristics of the aardvark (fig 7.13). Admittedly, the animal does not look too convincingly like its living counterpart but it has a long pointed nose, largish ears, a very small tail and very peculiar feet with exaggerated digits. The feet bear no resemblance to the same author's carnivore or ungulate feet. From their appearance, it seems reasonable to suppose that they are meant to represent strong digging feet with pronouncedly separate digits. The aardvark has very characteristic feet, differing from all other living mammals in having small hoofs on the digits, adapted for digging out the termites' nests on which the animal feeds. The front feet each have four hoofed digits, the hind feet five. Le Testu's animal has quite distinctly four digits in the front feet, one smaller, as in life, than the other three and it has

Fig 7.13 (over) South Africa from Le Testu's *Cosmographie Universelle* 1555 in the Bibliothèque Nationale, Paris: rhinoceros, lion, aardvark, camels, cinnamon bird, ostrich, snake, flying snake and elephant

at least four if not five in the hind. An animal with a somewhat similar appearance and soulful eyes occurs on Prunes' map of 1586 and corresponds well with a modern description of the aardvark: 'the ears are not unlike those of a donkey, the muzzle looks like a trombone, and the rather large eyes always have a somewhat soulful expression and fine long lashes' (Sanderson 1955).

Among the birds, the most obviously representative of the ethiopian region are the ostriches, which belong to an order confined to the region. They represent Africa through the centuries, varying in the realism of their portrayal though, mainly, accurate in their two toes. With the secretary bird, which appears rarely on the maps, they are the only endemic bird family that can be indisputably recognised on the maps, though parrots and birds of prey appear regularly.

RESEMBLANCES TO THE NEOTROPICAL REGION

Large flightless birds, resembling ostriches, also occur on maps of South America. These are the rheas which on the maps are usually correctly distinguished from the ethiopian ostriches by the number of toes. The rhea has three toes.

For long, the presence of rheas in South America and ostriches in Africa was thought to be proof of the close similarity of the neo-tropical and ethiopian faunas and, on the strength of this and on certain similarities in reptiles, amphibia, fish and the supposed close-ness of the two groups of monkeys, the two continents were thought to have formed part of one land mass during the early cenozoic. As a result of drifting apart (du Toit 1937, Runcorn 1962, Creer 1964) or as a result of the submergence of an atlantic continent (Buffon 1776), the present separation had been brought about. But, the two groups of monkeys are not closely related though sharing a common ancestor somewhere near the base of the primate stock and, although it is much debated, it seems likely that the ostriches and rheas are the result of parallel evolution to occupy the similar ecological niches of open grassland. Major changes in the relationships of these two southern continents have probably not occurred during the cenozoic, of some seventy million years. It seems more likely that most of their modern vertebrate fauna has arrived from the north: from the palearctic and oriental for the ethiopian region, from the nearctic region for the neotropical (George 1962).

CENOZOIC HISTORY

It seems likely that Africa became separated from all other continents during the cretaceous, having received only a few mammalian migrants, such as insectivores and condylarths. During the period of separation, probably until late eocene days, the insectivores could radiate into the several forms known today and the condylarths founded the elephant stock and probably the little changed aardvarks. Ancestors of modern monkeys and apes arrived during this time.

With the rejoining of the continent to the north early in the cenozoic, Africa was free to receive early carnivore stock and rodents and free to send out her elephant stock and primates (fig 7.14). Gradually the land connexion between Africa and the north dried, forming once more a barrier to faunal interchange, so that little migration took place after the pliocene. By that time, elephants had returned in more modern form, modern antelopes and horses were established and the rhinoceroses had come down from the north. The bears were a family that evolved too late to make the journey, an absence which made an impression on F. Alvares in 1520: 'except two which I never saw or heard tell that there are any of them here, bears and rabbits' (Beckingham & Huntingford 1961–1962). There are hares

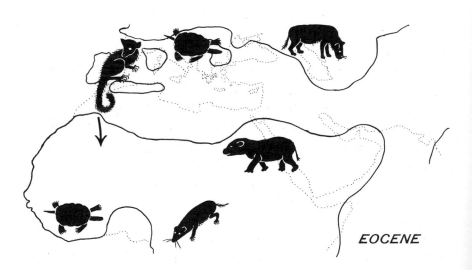

EOCENE

Fig 7.14 Hypothetical state of North Africa in the eocene about sixty million years ago: ancestors of elephants and African insectivores; primates migrate along the island chains from the palearctic

but, otherwise, only introduced European rabbits in Africa. But it is less clear why the deer were excluded, though it may be that the antelopes, arriving first, had already occupied all the niches suitable for fast moving cloven hoofed herbivores.

Thus, the fauna of the ethiopian region differs from the oriental region, because it was cut off from the rest of the Old World in the early stages of the cenozoic, but resembles the oriental because it had a channel of communication with it from oligocene to pliocene days (Arambourg 1964). It differs from the other tropical area of the world, the neotropical, both in the timing of its isolation and in its position in contact with the palearctic and oriental as distinct from the nearctic.

The resultant differences and similarities with other regions are reasonably well indicated on the maps. Its affinities with the oriental on the maps have already been indicated, by the appearance of five out of the eight shared families and, at the same time, its difference from this region is indicated by the occasional hippopotamus and ostriches which, correctly, do not appear in the cartographers' oriental region.

It is differentiated from the palearctic maps by lack of the commonly occurring bears and deer of that region and allied to it by horses from among the four families the regions share.

It is differentiated dramatically from the neotropical by, for instance, the large herbivores of the two regions, elephants and rhinos in the ethiopian compared with tapirs and llamas in the neotropical. But, tropical similarities are stressed in the appearance of snakes, dragons and monkeys in the two regions and, among birds, by the parrots and the large grazing flightless birds, ostriches and rheas.

In spite of their considerable success in typifying the ethiopian region, the cartographers portrayed only a maximum of thirteen of the thirty eight families of land mammals of the region, thirty four per cent, although the actual abundance of a variety of animals on any one map is as outstanding as some of the North American maps. This is particularly true of the Dutch maps like the Blaeu map in the *Klencke Atlas* about 1660 in the British Museum (fig 7.15).

Fig 7.15 (over) The ethiopian fauna on a map of Africa by Blaeu in the *Klencke Atlas* about 1660 in the British Museum, London

VIII

Australian Region

The australian region includes, with the large continent of Australia itself, some of the easterly islands of the Malay Archipelago.

WALLACE'S LINE

The exact boundary with the oriental region, among these islands, has been in dispute since Sclater first divided the world into the modern regions in 1858. The initiative for drawing the line was taken by A. R. Wallace who, travelling among the islands, studying the fauna, gradually assigned each to an area depending, largely, on how evident the australian element appeared to be on each island (Wallace 1864). Thus, because he met with white cockatoos, an essentially australian genus of the parrot family, and several other australian birds on Lombok, Wallace put the island of Lombok into the australian region and left Bali, only twenty one miles to the west, in the oriental region. Similarly, the presence of a pouched mammal, the cuscus *Phalanger,* on Celebes, many endemic species of other mammals, of birds and insects and the absence of typical western forms put this island into the australian region. In 1863, he drew the line that came to be called Wallace's line, running to the east of the Philippines and Borneo and southwards between Bali and Lombok.

During the hundred years that have elapsed, the line has been continually disputed and many others have been drawn that purported to divide the two faunas more satisfactorily (George 1964a). Weber's line, much further to the east, is the one that has persisted as the main rival to Wallace's line (Pelseneer 1904). The dispute over these two lines stresses the essential nature of the problem: that the middle islands of the archipelago have never been in direct land connexion with either of the great land masses to the east and to the west and have, therefore, been colonised in a haphazard way from across the sea. Population pressure, seemingly more severe in the oriental region, has tended to force more western animals on to the islands than australian. The boundary lies somewhere among these islands but, whatever criterion is used, at least New Guinea and the Aru Islands form part of the australian region and, almost certainly, the northern Moluccas. Timor is marginal and the rest are, probably, more oriental than australian. Wallace himself, eventually, put Celebes into the oriental region, in 1910.

TRAVELLERS' TALES

The exact position of the australian boundary is of little importance in studying the distribution of animals on maps because there are very few maps of either the islands of the Malay Archipelago or of Australia with animals on them. The years of cartographic animal abundance had passed before the coastlines of the islands and the continent in the australian region became known to explorers and mapmakers. Before the region was well known, however, many of the spice islands in the Malay Archipelago had been visited and reported on by traders and explorers. Journals of voyages to the Moluccas and other islands east of Wallace's line record the fauna. The fauna of islands tends to be less abundant than that of a continent and so, probably for this reason, the faunal picture that emerges from the journals is slight, compared with the picture that emerged from reports by visitors to South America.

In the Middle Ages, the oriental islands of Sumatra and, possibly, Borneo and Java were known, by hearsay, to travellers journeying to the far east. Marco Polo reported rhinoceroses, elephants, monkeys and many different birds from this area and, two centuries later, Vasco da Gama 1497–1499 was impressed by parrots as red as fire in the Malay peninsula (Ravenstein 1898).

The first report of animals from further east came from the Venetian, Nicolo de Conti, who described parrots from the island of Banda, in 1444 (Penzer 1937).

It was not until the sixteenth century, however, that reliable reports came from landfalls on other easterly islands of the archipelago.

The Portuguese reached the Moluccas in 1512 and the islands of
Aru and Timor soon afterwards. They touched New Guinea in 1526.
The Spanish discovered the Solomon Islands in 1567. But, although
the Portuguese or Dutch may have made landfalls on New Holland
in the early part of the sixteenth century (Margry 1867, Sharp 1963),
it was not until 1642 that a reliable description of a southern continent
came from Tasman to be followed, another fifty years later, by
Dampier.

Of the fauna, it was the birds that impressed the early travellers.
Nicolo de Conti reported: 'there be three kinds of popiniayes or
parrots, with redde feathers, and yellow billes, and others of divers
couloures, whiche are called *Nores* [lories], that is to say, cleare.
They are as bigge as doves. There be other white ones as bigge as
Hennes, named *Cachos*, that is to say, better, for they exceed the
others' (Penzer 1937). These are almost certainly the white cockatoos
Cacatua, considered so typical of the australian region since Wallace
designated their presence as indicative of his having crossed the
boundary line into the region from the oriental (Wallace 1869).

Tomé Pires 1512–1515 reported birds of paradise from the Aru
Islands and nose parrots or lories *Trichoglossus* from the Papuan
islands: 'The nose parrots come from the island of Papua. Those
which are prized more than any others come from the islands called
Aru, birds which they bring over dead, called birds of paradise,
and they say they come from heaven, and that they do not know
how they are bred' (Cortesão 1944). Various narratives, relating
to the discovery of the Solomon Islands, reported white cockatoos
and many and various other parrots. 'Parrots of all colours,' wrote
an anonymous traveller in 1586, 'like those of the other Indies of the
North. Other parrots entirely white, with a crest of feathers on their
heads the same as the *Calybaxa*, but with no other colour; they are
very tame, and never fierce' (Amherst & Thomson 1901).

Large pigeons, birds of prey and megapodes or brush turkeys,
geese and pheasants had also been noted. In 1568, Catoira had written:
'there are white and green and red and tawny mottled parrots
[eclectus parrot *Larius rosatus*], some like magpies [cuckoo tailed
parrots *Alisteris chloropterus*] and others of many colours. And there
are turkeys [megapodes] and pheasants, and eagles, and other birds
of prey, and very large ring-doves, and some have a very red fleshy
substance like cherries above their beaks [Papuan hornbills *Aceros*

plicatus perhaps], and their feathers are like the neck of a peacock' (Amherst & Thomson 1901). Not surprisingly, the varieties of parrots and pigeons attracted attention, for they are more numerous in the australian region than anywhere else in the world.

As well as birds, huge bats, the flying foxes or fruit bats, mice, dingo dogs, deer and domesticated pigs were reported from the islands.

THE IDENTIFICATION OF AUSTRALIA

From the early years of the sixteenth century, the existence of a large continent, seemingly south of Sumatra and Java, had been strongly suspected and referred to as Java la Grande. Its identity has given rise to much discussion ranging from the view of Hervé 1955 that the Java la Grande of the Dieppe maps 1542–1546 represents the mainland of Australia to Sharp 1963 identifying the same land mass with modern Java. Jean Fonteneau (Jean Alfonse de Saintonge) 1544 is presumed to have been describing this Java la Grande when he attempted to fix the geographical position of Tersye. 'Orfye est une isle et est en la mer Paciffique. Et Tersye est terre ferme, et est aussi en la coste de la mer Paciffique . . . et ainsi fut perdue la mémoire de Tersye et Orfye, et jusques à présent n'en a esté autre chose sçure, que l'on la serche tous les ans et qu'elle est en Oriant en la mer Paciffique. Ladicte mer Paciffique est toute plaine d'isles et d'autres grandes terres que l'on ne sçait si sont isles.'

Jean Fonteneau described some animals of Tersye: 'et en cette terre y a force d'or et d'argent et éléfans, et y a singes comme en la Barberie . . . et je me doubte que soit terre ferme et qu'elle va se joindre a la terre Australe' (Musset 1904).

It should be possible to argue that identification of the land in question can be made from the description of the fauna (George 1964*b*).

Elephants are not indigenous to either Australia or Java but they occur on Sumatra. Monkeys occur on both Java and Sumatra but the pig tailed macaques, which resemble most closely the Barbary apes, are found on Sumatra and not Java (Ellerman & Morrison-Scott 1951). The combination of elephants and pig tailed macaques makes it almost certain, on faunistic evidence, that Fonteneau was describing Sumatra. This can be further supported by the reference Fonteneau makes to the large quantity of gold. As long ago as 1535, Andres de

M

Urdaneta had identified Sumatra as an island of gold. 'From Sumatra they bring more gold than from any other part whatever, and it is very fine gold' (Markham 1911).

Unfortunately, the same sort of argument cannot be applied to the maps themselves, because so few animals occur on the islands. Terra Incognita tends to be filled up with familiar animals from other parts of the world. Thus, camels, deer, elephants, lions, some birds and lizards or crocodiles occupy La Terre Australe of the Desceliers' maps of the early middle sixteenth century. The presence of these more or less oriental animals would not seem to support the identification of this southern land mass with the mainland of Australia. The animals do not, however, help in making a choice between identifying Java or Sumatra as La Terre Australe. Elephants are not native to Java but they are to Sumatra; but elephants have been so widely domesticated that it would be difficult to justify the identification of an island solely on their presence or absence. The other animals could occur on either of the islands except, of course, the camels that come into the same category as the elephants: domestic animals which have been introduced as far as Australia itself.

To the Desceliers' fauna of La Terre Australe can be added a dog, a domestic horse and a tortoise with a long tail from the Vallard atlas of 1547.

In 1555, Le Testu depicted a curious collection of animals in Terre Australle (fig 8.1). There is a lion, an antlered deer, a crocodile, unicorns, dogs, cattle, parrots, a large flightless bird, a possible swan, a pig and a peculiar looking mammal.

Large flightless birds are typical of all the southern continents so that it may be that Le Testu was filling his southern continents with anything that seemed characteristic of the tropics, like the crocodiles and parrots, for example. By 1555, ostriches had been known from Africa for centuries and rheas had been depicted on the 1529 Ribeiro map of the world in South America. But equally, the large flightless cassowaries had already been reported from the australian islands. 'There is here a bird the size of a crane,' wrote Antonio Galvano in 1537, 'which cannot fly, not having wings sufficient for flight; but they run like a stag. With the feathers of this

Fig 8.1 Terre Australe from Le Testu's *Cosmographie Universelle* 1555 in the Bibliothèque Nationale, Paris

bird they adorn the heads of their idols' (Burney 1803–1817). Le Testu had flightless birds in all three southern continents on his maps, which makes it difficult to decide between distinct knowledge of rhea, ostrich and cassowary and a general use of large birds to characterise the south lands.

The peculiar mammal of the *Cosmographie* has carnivore feet, long ears and a long nose with prominent squared off teeth and goggle eyes. It has some resemblance to other drawings of a tapir but, as the oriental tapir was not discovered until the nineteenth century, it seems unlikely to be a representation of this animal. Equally, the australian marsupial mammals were not then known. A picture of the Malay sun bear could be read into this animal or even a dingo dog but this is being as imaginative as Le Testu for, almost certainly, this animal is of his imagination, but whether it was portrayed as an indication of ignorance of a land that might well contain extraordinary unknown animals or whether it was purely decorative must remain undecided. It may be significant that Le Testu himself wrote: 'la terre du sud, dite australe, laquelle n'a point encore été decouverte . . . pour ce n'est marquée que par l'imagination.'

Although a somewhat haphazard mixture of animals, the maps of the first part of the sixteenth century gave a reasonable representation of some of the islands of the Malay Archipelago: it was a fauna characteristic of tropical regions rather than peculiarly australian. Only the parrots, large flightless birds and, possibly, the long tailed turtle could be considered as representative of islands near Australia. Long tailed turtles are not particularly characteristic of far eastern lands, being found equally in North America. However, a long tailed smooth shelled animal *Platysternum* occurs in south China and, in northern Australia and New Guinea, the peculiar snake necks occur. They have very short tails but very long necks unlike any other turtles. It is just possible that Vallard's drawing is meant to represent one of these turtles, whose nearest relatives live in South America. In spite of this identification, these so-called australian animals are, equally, elements of any tropical fauna. This faunal generalisation would seem to derive from the geographical generalisation, based on a misinterpretation of Marco Polo (Skelton 1958), that a large land mass existed across the whole of the souther part of the world. 'J'estime,' wrote Fonteneau, 'que ceste coste [Magellan Straits] de la mer océane qu'est dicte coste Australe se va rendre en Orient a la

Jave, de coste d'occident de ladicte Jave' (Musset 1904). This description was carried out graphically in many of the maps of this period, Mercator's world map of 1569 (Bagrow 1964) and Wytfliet's of 1597 (see Wytfliet 1605), for example.

Ten years after Le Testu's spectacular contribution, a doubtful addition was made by Forlani. A rhinoceros, goat and dragon are combined with camel, lion, monkey, unicorn and elephant in his Terra Incognita but, significantly, while the camel, lion and monkey are below South America, the one horned rhino, goat, dragon, unicorn and elephant are below Africa and India, leaving the australian region, proper, without a fauna.

The following year, 1566, Le Testu made an important addition. A bird of paradise appears for the first time.

BIRDS OF PARADISE

This native australian bird flies, over the eastern half of the Le Testu world map, in company with a pheasant and a hornbill, both typically oriental, and they are contrasted with the grouse and quail of the western hemisphere (fig 9.3). Le Testu's bird of paradise had wings and long wiry feathers in its tail which, curiously, did not conform with current descriptions of the birds. Pigafetta described them, in 1521: 'These birds are as large as thrushes and have a small head and a long beak. Their legs are a palm in length and as thin as a reed and they have no wings, but in their stead long feathers of various colours like large plumes. Their tail resembles that of a thrush. All the rest of the feathers except the wings are tawny colour. They never fly except when there is a wind. The people told us that these birds came from the terrestrial paradise, and they call them Bolondivata, that is to say "birds of God"' (Robertson 1906).

Both Le Testu's figure and Pigafetta's description apply to either the great bird of paradise *Paradisea apoda* or the lesser bird of paradise *Paradisea minor*, both of which are dark bodied with, in the male, brilliant yellow or orange wing feathers and have two wiry feathers in the tail, very long in the great bird of paradise. In spite of Pigafetta's description, Le Testu gives his bird wings, in sharp contrast to the drawings that had already been seen in Gesner's *Historiae Animalium* in 1551 (fig 8.2) and Belon's *Portraits d'oyseaux* in 1557. Belon was describing the fauna and flora of Egypt and Arabia and, interestingly, uses Gesner's picture of a bird of paradise as an illustration of a phoenix, a tradition that seems to have continued because, in 1605, Wytfliet also reported from the Moluccas birds of paradise that resembled the phoenix. Gesner, however, calls it Paradise avis, Manucodiata, Avicula Dei, Paradysvogel or Luftvogel.,

Some years later, however, the map pictures catch up with the bestiaries and the wings as well as the feet have disappeared from the bird of paradise:

Here are these golden Birds which to the ground
Never descend, and only dead are found

(Camöens 1572, translated by Fanshawe 1655). On Bertelli's map of Asia 1567, published by Ortelius, there is such a bird of paradise (fig 8.3).

Ortelius' bird of paradise flew out of New Guinea, a mass of soft

Fig 8.2 The great bird of paradise from Gesner's *Historiae Animalium* 1551

Fig. 8.3 (right) *Carta dele' Asia* by Bertelli 1567: the bird of paradise is without legs and has the two wire feathers in its tail

feathers, with neither feet nor wings but in its tail were the two characteristic wire feathers, absent from Gesner's picture. In line with this drawing is the description, by Linschoten, in the 1598 English translation of *Itinerario*: '. . . in these islands onlie is found the bird, which the Portingales call passaros de Sol, that is Fowle of the Sunne, the Italians call it Manucodiatas, and the Latinists, Paradiseas, and by us called Paradice birds, for ye beauty of their feathers which passe all other birds: these birds are never seene alive, but being dead they are found upon the Iland: they flie, as it is said alwaies into the Sunne, and keepe themselves continually in the ayre without lighting on the earth, for they have neither feet nor wings, but onely head and body, and the most part tayle, as appeareth by the birdes that are brought from thence into India' (Burnell & Tiele 1885).

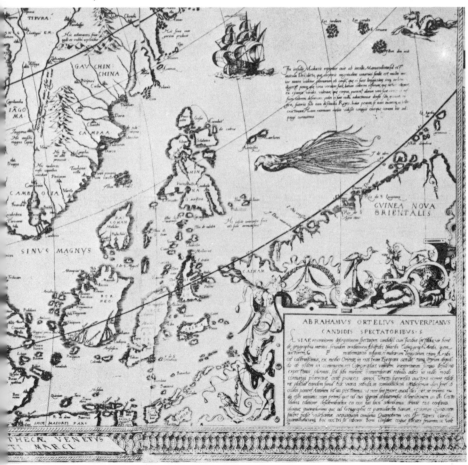

The great Spanish naturalist Acosta, a few years earlier, was non-committal about wings but found a function for the two long tail feathers although conventionally depriving the birds of feet. 'Certaine birds from China that have no fete, and all their bodies are almost feathers. They sit not upon the ground, but hang upon boughs, by strings or feathers which they have, and so rest themselves like flies or airie things.'

Before the close of the century, another version had appeared, in an inset to Petrus Plancius' *Magellanica*, in 1594. This bird had wings but, ostentatiously, no feet and lacked the typical wire tail feathers of the previous maps (fig 8.4). This bird reappears, from time to time, on the maps of the seventeenth century: Speed, in 1631, for example. And in a later edition of Speed there is added yet another piece of information about the birds: 'the Henne layeth her eggs (if you will believe it) in a hole of the Cockes back' (Speed 1646).

The birds of paradise were greatly prized by the spice traders but they had never seen them alive, as they were brought from the interior of New Guinea, Australia or some of the neighbouring small islands already prepared for sale, with feet and sometimes wings removed and intestines replaced by preservative spices. The practice of cutting off the feet was so common and the live birds so rare that, in 1758, Linnaeus gave to the great bird of paradise the definitive name *Paradisea apoda*, at the same time noting, however, that it was wrongly said to be without feet. Buffon, in 1775, maintained that they had neither feet nor intestines. It was only a few years later that live birds were exhibited in Europe and accurate pictures became available (Goldsmith 1776, Pennant 1791, Levaillant 1806).

The complete bird never appears on the maps.

PARROTS AND POUCHED MAMMALS

The Pasterot *Livre de la Marine* of 1587 adds little to the map fauna. The by now usual deer and parrots occur with domestic animals across an extended southern continent. Pasterot adds basilisks and other birds of prey. The presence of a swan in the australian region of his atlas tends to confirm the swan of Le Testu's 1555 map. The black swan *Chenopis atrata* is a species native to Australia and could reasonably be considered typical of the region, even though its near relatives are known from the northern regions and from South America (Delacour & Mayr 1945).

Up to the end of the century, then, only parrots, snake neck turtles, birds of paradise, swans and a large flightless bird had appeared on the maps from among the native australian fauna already reported in the travellers' journals. The deer, large cats and rhinoceroses that were depicted in the southern land are not animals of the australian region but typical of the more westerly islands and continent of the oriental region. The domestic animals were not distinguishable from anywhere else.

Although parrots had occurred frequently they did not acquire the distinctive forms of cockatoos and lories until an inset in a map by Allardt in about 1652 (Coote 1895) and on the later Coronelli globes 1688–1696. Pigeons which, like the parrots, reach their greatest diversity in the australian region, were not distinguishable until the same Allardt map. Flying foxes, so often reported by the explorers, did not gain the status of map animals.

The seventeenth century saw an increase in the knowledge of the fauna of the australian region but this increase in knowledge was not transferred to the maps of the period. Diego de Prado y Tovar 1605–1606 describing the fauna of New Guinea noted the many wondrous different parrots, the bats, cassowaries and other birds and the Papuan dogs (possibly dingos). He added to Galvano's description of a cassowary the interesting habits: 'it ate pebbles, iron tarpauling nails, pieces of linen and paper and when it drank sea-water it got drunk, and then it was a sight to see the leaps and

Fig 8.4 Bird of paradise from Petrus Plancius' *Magellanica* 1594 in Linschoten's *Itinerario*

springs it made in the ship.' And, before this, Diego de Prado y Tovar had reported: 'here we killed an animal which is in the shape of a dog smaller than a greyhound, with a bare and scaly tail like that of a snake, and his testicles hang from a nerve like a thin cord, they say that it was the castor, we ate it and it was like venison, its stomach was full of ginger leaves and for that reason we ate it' (Stevens & Barwick 1930). Thus, by 1606, a marsupial mammal had been reported from the australian region (George 1964*c*) though not identified as such nor recognised as having any affinities with the opossum known from South America since 1499.

It seems likely that Prado's *Relación* was not well known to any but the Spaniards and the discovery of this new animal, probably one of the scrub wallabies *Thylogale* (Marlow 1965, Calaby 1965, George 1965), was not widely reported. Pelsaert, in 1629, discovered another marsupial, either one of the phalangers or another wallaby (Troughton 1941).

Neither the kangaroo nor the pouched phalangers appeared on any of the maps which is, perhaps, not surprising, since a wallaby was not reported again until Dampier's voyages of 1697–1703: the hare wallaby *Lagostrophus*, according to Troughton. The first kangaroo (red kangaroo or the whip tail wallaby) was not drawn until some seventy years later, as a result of the Cook expeditions (Beaglehole 1955). Not until the nineteenth century was it realised that the australian region held a fauna of pouched mammals unique in its variety, together with the only egg-laying mammals of the world. Buffon even doubted whether pouched mammals could occur anywhere but South America, where they were represented by opossums; he suggested, in 1763, that the report of a pouched phalanger from the island of Amboyna was either incorrect or that the animal had been imported from somewhere else.

Neither the mapmakers nor the naturalists were any more familiar with the australian fauna than they were with the contours of the land in the region.

THE COLONISATION OF THE AUSTRALIAN REGION

In the early years of the cenozoic, marsupials were widespread across the northern hemisphere though, today, they are found only in the neotropical, nearctic and australian regions. It is comparatively easy to account for their presence in South America. What is less easy to understand is why they should be almost the only mammals to get to Australia.

During the early years of their radiation they were not the only mammals in the world, as some have thought. Besides the egg-laying mammals, whose peregrinations are even more obscure, owing to lack of fossil evidence, there were in cretaceous and paleocene days a number of insectivore placental mammals, as well as the early opossum-like marsupials. All these mammals occurred in the northern hemisphere, the nearctic and palearctic regions. There was free access to Africa from the palearctic, until some time in the cretaceous; but it seems that South America was not joined to North America and Australia was not joined to Asia by continuous land at this time. It must be presumed that a string of islands was the only connexion with Australia but this does not explain why marsupials made the island hops and the placentals did not. It seems possible that early marsupials were more arboreal than their insectivore contemporaries and were, therefore, more likely to be swept from island to island on rafts of trees and vegetation. Once in Australia, they radiated widely to fill most of the continent's ecological niches. Once established, they could repel any later chance immigrant of placental stock, with the exception of a few rats, bats and the dingo dog (Simpson 1961).

The mammalian colonisation of Australia has been more haphazard than that of the other southern continents, its fauna differs from the rest of the world more than that of any other continent and its definitive discovery by man was delayed for some two centuries after the great adventurers opened up the New World.

Its discovery was too late for the fauna to be attractive to the map-makers.

IX

World Maps

The foregoing survey of the zoogeography of the world as seen on maps was based not only on complete maps of the world but also on the individual maps of atlases and on maps made of more restricted localities. The conclusions reached are, therefore, those that could have been reached by anyone looking through these maps. No one map provided all the information nor were all the maps world maps.

MAPS OF THE WORLD

World maps, that portray animals, do not necessarily have all their regions filled with animals, so that some maps are not, strictly, representing the different faunas of the world but indicating the fauna of one or two regions. This is mainly true of the earlier maps, several of which have an occasional animal in Africa and none in the rest of the world although, generally, animals appear, if they appear at all, in both the ethiopian and the palearctic regions with only the oriental region consistently deprived of its fauna. Even so, at least five of the early maps are strictly zoogeographical maps, in the sense that they have a fauna for all three regions: the Ebstorf (fig 9.1), Hereford (fig 2.1) and Vercelli maps of the thirteenth century and the Borgia (fig 2.12) and Genoese (fig 2.8) world maps of the fifteenth century. The fourteenth century neglected the oriental region.

From these early 'distribution' maps, it could be learnt that, while snakes, dragons, birds, some carnivores and domestic camels were common to all regions; elephants, unicorns and crocodiles were shared by the ethiopian and oriental regions; leopards, pelicans and ostriches by the palearctic and ethiopian and that, while elk and bears were particularly representative of the palearctic, giraffes were peculiar to the ethiopian, along with rhinoceros and antelope which, however, occur only once.

As an attempt at mapping animals, these maps were only a partial success. They give a general, if sparse, idea of the fauna of the three regions, but they are not outstanding for the accuracy with which the animals are distributed. But the errors are, usually, those of omission: the animals tend not to have a wide enough range to satisfy accuracy. Only rarely do animals occur in the wrong region. Camels are the main offenders but, in the domesticated form, they have been used all over the Old World for centuries and their presence in all three regions is not, therefore, particularly misleading. It is interesting that, already, elephants had come, correctly, to represent the ethiopian and oriental regions and elk to represent the palearctic.

During the first half of the sixteenth century, interest turned to the New World but, in spite of the new discoveries, the fauna of the ethiopian region still held first place on world maps and in world atlases. Indeed, some maps populated only the ethiopian region, leaving the rest of the world blank, while others populated only the neotropical region. At least eight featured the fauna of both ethiopian and neotropical regions, disregarding the rest of the world. These eight maps seem to have been particularly concerned to emphasise the differences between the two great southern continents: elephants were primarily the typical animals of Africa; parrots and then, towards the middle of the century, opossums represented South America.

There were, however, several maps and atlases which gave a fauna to all five regions of the then known world and some also included the sixth, unknown, region. Several others covered at least four regions. These were mainly the work of the Dieppe school, the earliest of which to fall in this category is the 1536 Harleian or Dauphin map to be followed by, among others, the Desceliers, Vallard and Le Testu maps.

From early sixteenth century maps of the world, new facts could be added to the early distribution maps. The cat family of carnivores had taken on a world wide distribution whereas, earlier, they had been confined to the palearctic and ethiopian regions. The range of deer had been correctly extended to cover all regions, except the ethiopian. Bears retained their northerly distribution, but had been

Fig 9.1 The Ebstorf map of the world about 1235 from the Miller reproduction: animals in the palearctic bottom left; ethiopian bottom right; oriental region top

extended to the recently discovered nearctic region. Although the bear family does reach its greatest diversity in the north, which is probably its centre of origin, there are species of bears in both the neotropical and the oriental region. Elephants were still, accurately, confined to the ethiopian and oriental regions.

With the extension of knowledge of the land surface, new concepts of animal distribution were made clear. It became apparent, from the maps of the early sixteenth century, that some animals were discontinuously distributed. Such were the flightless birds, ostrich and rhea, occurring in the two large southern continents but absent from the intervening nearctic and palearctic regions. Monkeys are similarly shown on the maps, discontinuously distributed. They are shown mainly in the neotropical and ethiopian regions, with a few in the oriental. Again, other animals occur with a southerly but different distribution such as the rhinoceroses, which are always portrayed correctly in the ethiopian or oriental regions. Yet others have a wider but still discontinuous distribution such as the snakes and parrots, which turn up correctly in all the southern regions and are absent from the north.

Some of the regions could be further characterised on these maps by unique animals: animals occurring in only one region. The opossum, for instance, is shown as typical of the neotropical region (it has migrated into the United States only recently); the reindeer is made to symbolise the palearctic (although there are North American reindeer, caribou); a jungle fowl is correctly confined to the oriental and a giraffe continues to be confined to the ethiopian.

As the century advanced and knowledge increased, the main additions to the maps of the world were newly discovered animals such as armadillos and anteaters. The distribution of the well known groups hardly changes from the earlier years but is reinforced by reiteration.

Several world maps stand out for being of particular interest. The 1551 map of the world by the Spanish Royal cosmographer Sancho Gutiérrez is lavish with its animals (fig 9.2). In the New World, the southern continent has two sorts of llamas, alligators, monkey, macaws and other birds while the north has deer, bison, a coyote, jack rabbit and birds. In contrast, in the Old World, the southern continents have camel, elephant, ostrich, lion, tiger, unicorn, jackal, snake, dragons and cattle in the ethiopian and pheasant, boar, goats, jungle fowl, elephant, four horned goat or antelope and what is, probably, a bear in the oriental. The northern region of the Old World is typified by a reindeer and a stork. Thus, Gutiérrez indicated some similarity between the two northern temperate regions but contrasted the southern regions both with one another and with the north.

In 1566, Le Testu's map of the world is interesting in its emphasis on the overall difference between the Old World and the New World with less regard for precise localisation (fig 9.3). Thus, a bear stands in the nearctic, an armadillo and an anteater in the neotropical. Over the New World, in general, grouse and quail fly. In contrast, giraffe, lynx, deer, elephant and dragon stand indiscriminately over the northerly part of the Old World with a chameleon in the ethiopian region. Over the Old World fly pheasants, a hornbill and a bird of paradise.

José de Costa e Miranda's world map of 1706 is interesting more for its late date than for anything it adds to the knowledge of the fauna (fig 9.4). It follows the convention of deer in the north, armadillo in the neotropical, elephant in the oriental and monkey in the ethiopian region but, except for the Coronelli globe from the end of the seventeenth century, it stands alone, so late in time, as an essay in zoogeography.

It is interesting to compare these maps with modern attempts at portraying, in a small space, the distinctive features of the zoogeographical regions.

Termier and Termier 1960, for instance, show palearctic and nearctic sharing bears and deer, with bison in the nearctic and a Bactrian camel in the palearctic. Elephants represent both oriental and ethiopian, with the addition of giraffe and single humped camel in Africa. An armadillo and a llama are considered distinctive of the neotropical and a kangaroo of the australian.

A second example, a recent Italian map, in *Knowledge* 1965, well filled with animals, unites palearctic and nearctic with assorted deer, bears, marmots, squirrels, otters and wolves and, curiously, distinguishes between them by a beaver, an eagle and a Bactrian camel in the palearctic in contrast to polar bear, bison, musk ox, puma and lynx in the nearctic. The tropical regions on this map show mainly unique animals, except for the camel and cat family that link South America with temperate regions and the camel, horse and cat families

N

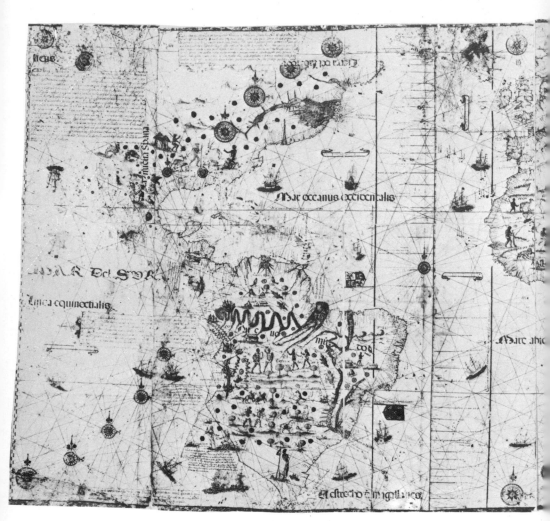

Fig 9.2 Gutiérrez map of the world 1551 in the Österreichische Nationalbibliothek, Vienna: animals in the neotropical, nearctic, palearctic,
ethiopian and oriental regions

that link Africa with the north. South America and Africa show resemblances in having representatives of the cat family and large
flightless birds. The ethiopian and oriental are united by elephants,
rhinoceroses, cats and apes and distinguished by giraffe, hippopotamus, antelope, crocodile and chameleon. Only eagles join
oriental and palearctic. The australian region has only crocodile,
lizard, kangaroo and sea lion.

It must be conceded that even though these modern maps were
drawn specially to show zoogeographical distribution, a subject

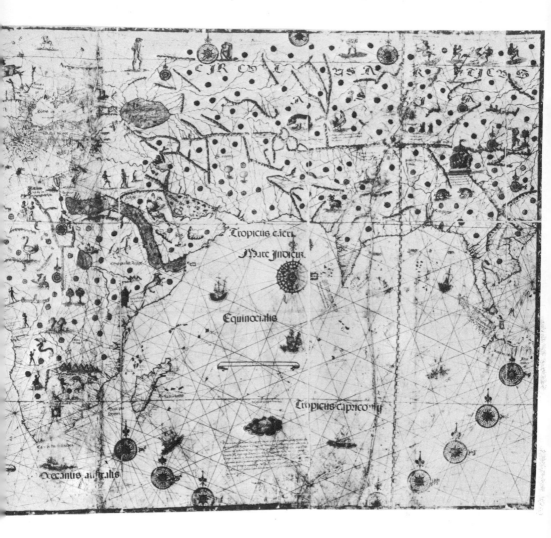

that hardly came into being until well on into the nineteenth century (Johnston 1848, Wallace 1876), they do little better than some of the ancient maps drawn for more general purposes.

ATLASES

After 1547, the animals of the world were drawn mainly on the separate maps of atlases rather than on world maps. Of particular interest are the atlases of Vallard 1547, Le Testu 1555, de Jode 1593, Linschoten's *Itinerario* 1596, the Mercator-Hondius atlas of 1606 and the Blaeu atlases and their copies from 1635 onwards. In all these collections of maps, either all or many of the maps have animals on them. They continue the trend of the world maps in their animal distribution and frequently add to the fauna. Turkeys and beavers become common in the nearctic, the neotropical fauna flourishes, the ethiopian acquires an extensive fauna particularly in the Blaeu maps in the *Klencke Atlas* (fig 7.15), for instance, rhinoceroses and elephants become common in the oriental region.

Modern distribution maps can be seen in *Animal Geography* (George 1962) where each geographical region is drawn as a separate map. Like the late sixteenth century and early seventeenth century atlases, a turkey distinguishes the nearctic from the palearctic, a camel the palearctic from the nearctic. Beavers, however, unite the two regions whereas, in the early atlases, the beavers were mainly confined to the nearctic. Rhinoceroses and pangolins unite oriental and ethiopian regions, aardvark and okapi, tapir and tarsier distinguish them. The neotropical region resembles the oriental in its tapir, the palearctic in its llamas, the ethiopian in its large flightless bird and is distinctive for sloths and armadillos. The australian region has, among several marsupial mammals, cassowary, cockatoo and tortoise. The variety of animals has increased, but the same basic types of the old maps have continued to be used in modern zoogeographical illustrations.

Animal distribution maps similar to the atlases can be found today among many tourist maps.

THE REGIONS CONTRASTED

On the world maps that have an abundance of animals and in the atlases, where several regions have animals on them, the emphasis is mainly on contrast between regions with the exception of the oriental and ethiopian regions, which are continually being shown with similar elephants, camels, rhinos and unicorns. To some extent, the palearctic and nearctic are shown to have similarity by sharing deer and bears. In general, however, it is rare to feature animals in common between regions. From the earliest times contrasts had been emphasised. The reindeer, elks and polar bears represented a northern temperate region in the Old World, the palearctic; in marked contrast to animals of the tropical regions further south, the elephants, rhinoceroses, snakes and lizards of the oriental and ethiopian.

This representation would seem to come directly from the interests in the south of the traders who had operated from these earliest times. In India and in Africa, they searched for or bartered for rhinoceroses, elephants, lions: elephants for war, lions for the Roman games; elephants to provide the valuable ivory of commerce, rhinoceros horns, snakes and lizards for the apothecary (Schoff 1912).

EXPLANATIONS OF THE DIFFERENCES

Naturalists had commented on the products of the ethiopian and oriental regions, observing both their similarities and their differences from one another and from the palearctic. Some had tried to offer an explanation of the phenomenon. Aristotle, in *Historia Animalium*, ascribed the faunal differences to climate, which was a not unreasonable interpretation of Old World differences. Pliny, in *Naturalis Historia*, expressed surprise at the facts but offered no explanation. Saint Augustine of Hippo, in *De Civitate Dei*, realising that it was difficult to reconcile animal distribution with the story of the Ark, suggested that most animals had been regenerated on the spot from the mud, but those that required two of a kind to copulate had been preserved in the Ark and then distributed to their present homes, either by man or carried through the air by angels.

The distribution question became more acute with the discovery of a totally unexpected fauna in the New World, during the sixteenth century. Both the naturalists and the cartographers could not but stress the differences between the Old World and the New World, between northern regions and southern regions. The differences between Africa and South America were stressed by the absence of elephants, rhinoceroses and camels from the neotropical region, by the absence from the ethiopian of opossums, anteaters, peccaries, armadillos and llamas, for instance. Beavers and turkeys occupied North America, reindeer and elks Eurasia. But the increasing trade in fur skins from Russia and from North America also helped to stress similarities between the two northern temperate regions. This made the differences between South America and Africa even more striking and more puzzling.

Acosta, in *Historia Natural y Moral de las Indias* 1596, a book popular throughout western Europe, raised the problem of differential animal distribution when describing, with considerable accuracy, the fauna and flora of South America. Initially, he thought, the animals

Fig 9.3 (over)· Le Testu's map of the world 1566 in the Bibliothèque Nationale, Paris

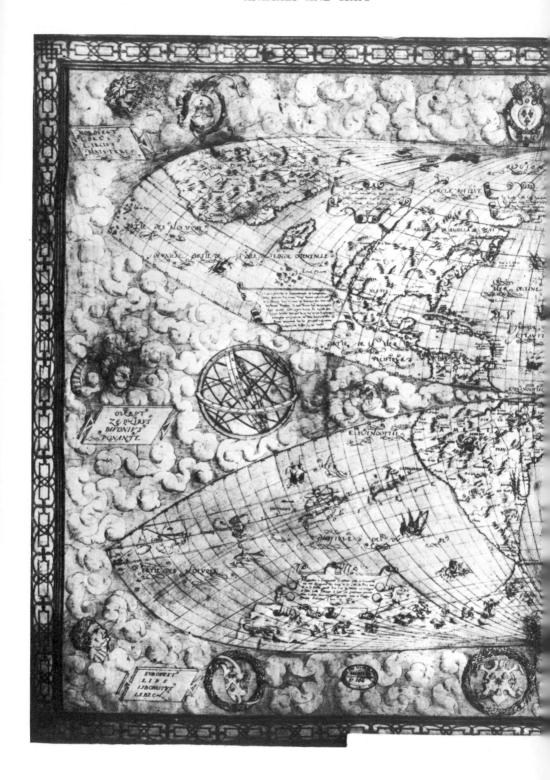

of the various regions had been created but, for him, the question still remained as to how they had got to America and Africa after being collected together in the Ark. Some might be new creations but the others must have travelled. He dismissed swimming as impossible and decided they must have travelled by land and he observed that the extent of the land towards the north pole and the south pole was not known, so that it was reasonable to suppose that the land was continuous and, therefore, provided a migration route. Small changes, from time to time, in the form of the north and south lands, however, altered the usefulness of the routes. Some animals could migrate across them, others could not. This was a view held by some cartographers of the time. For instance, Le Testu 1566 had an inhabited land to the south (fig 9.3), virtually continuous with South America and Australia and Camocio, in 1569, showed that North America and Asia connected across the Bering Straits. Others were less committed to north and south connexions: Ribeiro 1529, Mercator 1587, 1595, for example (Bagrow 1964).

Acosta's solution was not generally acceptable though his question retained its validity; many others continued to query why there were no elephants in South America (Thomas Browne 1643, Robert Burton 1628) but gave no answer. By this time, even greater problems were foreshadowed. The far eastern traders were bringing back, with their main cargo of spices, new varieties of parrots and the birds of paradise, unknown from anywhere else in the world. Gradually, too, reports came in of peculiar hopping mammals with prominent testicles and pouches for their young.

Buffon 1749–1766 returned to the challenge, setting out in detail the general mammalian characteristics of the New World and the Old World. In 1761, he contrasted the tapirs, peccaries, anteaters, llamas, opossums, agoutis and armadillos of the southern New World with the elephants, rhinoceroses, hippopotamuses, giraffes, camels, hyenas and chevrotains of the Old World, for instance, remarking that the monkeys of the two continents were different. Secondly, he noted that the two continents had some animals in common, though rarely of the same species. He resolved the problem in much the same way as Acosta but went further. Animals had been able to migrate between the continents, across the north between Asia and North America and, at some times in the past, between Africa and South America across what is now the south Atlantic Ocean. But the sea had separated the continents before they had exchanged all their animals. Separated, the animals became different because of the different conditions on the different continents. 'Nature, I avow, is in a state of continual flux; but it is enough for man to seize the moment of his own century and to throw a few looks backwards and a few forward, to try to see what it was once like, and what it might eventually become.'

By Buffon's time, the cartography of the world was nearly complete. It seemed unlikely that there was continuous land either in the north or the south so it was necessary for him to suppose that this was something that had been in the past and was no longer true. This introduced an idea of change so, if change in the land, why not change in the animals themselves. In the main, however, creation held the day and few such disturbing questions were considered.

It was not until the nineteenth century that revolutionary thought on the distribution of animals became generally accepted.

Lyell 1830–1833 first established that while continents had always had some sort of identity related to the ones known today they had also undergone gradual change in detail, they had evolved. There could, therefore, have been connexions between continents which no longer exist today.

Darwin 1859 argued for the gradual evolution of animals by natural selection and used, as one of the arguments in its favour, the seemingly anomalous distribution of animals round the world. Natural processes, it seemed, had brought about the irregularity.

Wallace, 1876 and earlier, combined the theories of evolution of continents and evolution of animals by natural selection into the modern theory of zoogeography. Briefly, he argued that both continents and animals had changed during time. Thus, when two continents were connected they could exchange animals, when they were separated they could not. They could exchange only those animals that existed at the particular time in question. Modern faunas, then, were the result of interchanges between different continents at different geological periods at different evolutionary stages.

This theory could suggest, for instance, that bears had not evolved in time to migrate into Africa while a habitable stretch of land joined that continent with the palearctic or the oriental. It could suggest that some animals like tapirs and camels had once been widespread but, owing to extinction in the middle of their range, were left with the

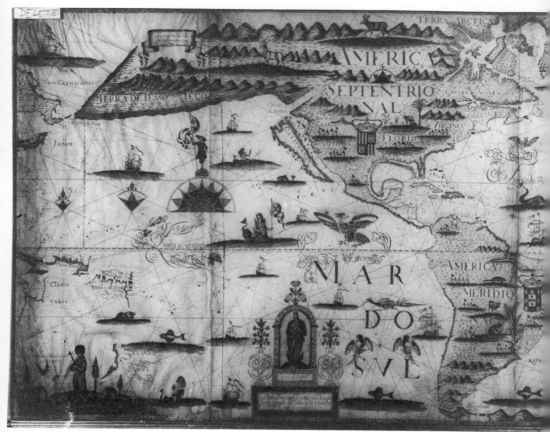

Fig 9.4 Map of the world 1706 by José de Costa e Miranda in the Mitchell Library, Sydney

discontinuous populations of today. The theories of evolution gave a dynamic aspect to animal distribution: animals, plants, continents and climate changed during time.

Simple migration at various epochs from the north southwards and from east to west was the basis of Wallace's thesis. It appeared to account well for the spectacular differences between the southern continents and for the similarities between the palearctic and nearctic.

Opponents, unable to refute this explanation of differences, concentrated on the similarities between widely distanced lands, demanding not why are there tapirs in South America and rhinoceroses in Africa, but why are there monkeys in the two continents? Why are the porcupines, ostriches, turtles, frogs and lungfish of the southern continents more closely related to one another than they are to the intervening northern forms? The stress had shifted from the differ-

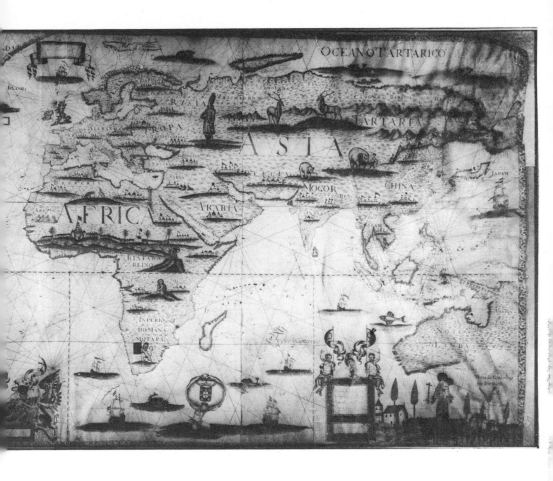

ences, which had found expression in the earlier naturalists' books and on the maps, to the similarities (George 1964a).

While many maps depict monkeys in either the one southern continent or the other or ostrich-like birds and parrots in either one or the other, only a few show them in both at the same time. The Cantino map of 1502 had parrots on both continents though contrasted by the long tails and bright colours of the South American forms. Desceliers 1546 had monkeys and ostrich-like birds in both southern continents. A few others showed either the ostriches or the monkeys in common.

To the cartographers of the sixteenth and seventeenth centuries, the neotropical and ethiopian regions were essentially different from one another and were to be contrasted.

This is probably a fair estimate of the situation. The differences are greater than the similarities. Even the apparent similarities of monkeys, porcupines and ostriches are less real than they might seem. As Buffon knew, the monkeys of the two continents differ markedly from one another and are almost certainly the result of parallel evolution, from a remote tarsier-like ancestor from the north, to fill the forest niche of the two tropical southern continents. The same sort of argument has been used, recently, to account for the porcupines which, in any event, occur today in the nearctic and palearctic as well as the south (Wood 1950).

The ostrich and rhea may also not be more closely related than any other modern birds (McDowell 1948). Parrots, of course, are widespread in their distribution, occurring in every region except the palearctic.

Although the simple concept of origin and evolution of the major groups in the northern land mass has been much modified in recent years (Pilgrim 1941, Darlington 1957, Clark 1959), the general thesis of migration through the northern regions to reach the southern, when the routes were open, still finds favour (Matthew 1915, Simpson 1953). It is, however, possible that a way once existed through a warmer Antarctic, but this has yet to be proved and would almost certainly have been too early, in geological time, to help the mammals or the birds (Simpson 1940). Further, it is possible that the continents have changed their positions relative to one another to a greater extent than had been believed and that the distribution problems are more complex than they would seem to be (Runcorn 1962, Creer 1964). This possibility of drifting continents has also still to be given proof and delineation but such an event, too, would probably be too early to be of use to mammals and birds, which were the main concern of the early cartographers and the early explorers.

It can be concluded that in expressing differences between Old World and New World and differences between tropical and temperate regions and picking on a few unique animals of the zoogeographical regions, the older cartographers provided an interesting and accurate lesson in the geographical distribution of animals.

X

Conclusion

As new lands were reported and appeared on the maps so new animals were written about and depicted on the maps. Many explorers wrote as much about the animals and plants of a region as they did about the people or the conformation of the coastline. Many of the cartographers used this information fully and their maps showed not only the shape of continents and islands but also many of the animals belonging to particular parts of the world. As new lands became more accurately and more fully delineated so more animals were to be found on the maps.

The continent of South America was reported in 1499 and the following year an attempt to depict such a continent occurred on the world map of Juan de la Cosa. Only two years later, the Cantino and Caveri maps showing the coastline of South America also showed long tailed parrots. By 1529, the configuration of the eastern part of the New World was reasonably well known and, by that date, Ribeiro had filled the South American continent with some fifteen different types of animal (fig 10.1); some, like deer, well known from other parts of the world; others, like armadillos and rheas, new to naturalists.

At the same time as the southern continent became known, explorers were reporting animals from North America but these animals were slower to appear on the maps. The Homem-Reinel maps of 1519 started with a few typical nearctic animals (bears, deer and coyotes) but increase was slow until the middle of the century when, on French maps, much of the definitive map fauna started to appear as a result, very largely, of the reports of Jacques Cartier.

It seems then that, whereas reports of discoveries of new lands, of coastlines or islands often travelled from one country to another rapidly to influence the cartographers, the incorporation of new animals into the map fauna was either slow or had to wait for direct contact between cartographer and explorer or his journal. Catalan maps of the late fourteenth and early fifteenth centuries, for example, derived at second hand from reports of Marco Polo's journeys, are as disappointing in their animals as the early maps of North America.

Accuracy of the animal drawings with consequent ease of identification gradually improved with a few outstanding exceptions. Hondius's armadillo is more obviously identifiable than Ribeiro's armadillo of sixty years earlier. Vallard's ethiopian elephants have more correct detail than the elephants of the Ebstorf or Hereford maps. Notable exceptions to this statement are the opossums and howler monkeys of the New World which, from reasonably accurate beginnings, became so formalised as to be unrecognisable in the seventeenth century, without knowing the sequence that led up to them.

In spite of these regressions, the trend is mainly one of improvement, both in the knowledge of the form of the animals themselves and in the overall representation of regional faunas. This improvement culminates, about the middle of the seventeenth century, in the work of the Dutch cartographers. But, after this, the decline in map faunas is rapid.

By the end of the seventeenth century, excluding the australian region which was hardly known, an average of twelve mammalian families had been represented in each region with a scattering of birds and reptiles. This number forms a considerable proportion of the total terrestrial mammalian fauna, if bats are excluded.

The nearctic region with a small total of twenty three families had scored thirteen on the maps, or fifty six per cent. The neotropical follows in abundance having the largest map total, fourteen: the larger number of families actually living on that continent, thirty one, puts the proportional representation down to forty five per cent. The palearctic follows with twelve out of twenty eight, forty three per cent. The oriental has eleven out of thirty, thirty seven per cent. Curiously, the ethiopian comes last with a possible thirteen out of thirty eight, thirty four per cent.

The low score of the ethiopian is probably largely because the total number of families now known from the region exceeds that of all others and partly because the large herbivores of the region were so spectacular as to overshadow the smaller carnivores and rodents which, in fact, make up a large part of the ethiopian fauna.

Care has been taken to underestimate rather than to overestimate the variety on the maps by excluding all but the reasonably certain identifications. Some of the smaller carnivores might represent civets and, thus, add another family to the count; but the identification is so unsure that they have not been included. Further, the figures are proportions of the terrestrial mammal families known today. Many of those missing from the maps, however, were either not known until long after animals had ceased to play a part on maps or were not known to inhabit a particular region. The obvious examples of the lack of such information were the tapirs, unknown from the oriental region until 1805 but whose close relatives had not only been known since the sixteenth century but had appeared on several maps of the neotropical region. It is doubtful whether, by the end of the seventeenth century, anyone had differentiated the nearctic pocket mice from ordinary mice or had reported jumping mice from North America. It is most unlikely that anyone had recognised in the nearctic the western mountain beaver as distinctive or had heard the pikas whistling in the mountains of either the nearctic or the palearctic. No one in Europe had seen the giant panda of China until 1870 (Edwards 1868–1874) and so the raccoon family, to which it belongs, could not be represented on Old World maps.

But lack of information does not account for all the omissions. Gophers had been reported in writing by Drake 1578 (Hakluyt 1589) and so, too, had the New World raccoons (Topsell 1658) but they are not distinguishable in the map faunas.

Making a rough estimate of the families that had been recorded from well known books on animals of the period some idea can be gained of the proportion of the then known animals that were seen on maps. From Gesner *Historiae Animalium* 1551 and later editions, supplemented by Acosta *Historia Natural y Moral de las Indias* 1589 and translations up to 1604, late editions of Topsell *The History of Four-Footed Beasts* 1607–1658 and a few travellers' diaries, a new total can be arrived at.

Thus, there is no indication that the neotropical marsupial mice

were known to these authorities (they were identified in the nineteenth century) nor is it clear whether they had distinguished between
the families of New World tree porcupines and the families of Old
World ground porcupines and precisely the same doubt hangs over
the map porcupines and the writings of many later naturalists. About
eight of the twelve South American rodent families seem to have been
identified by the end of the seventeenth century: at least four have
been recorded on the maps. This adjustment makes the proportion
represented for the neotropical fifty six per cent.

The same sort of argument eliminates pikas, pocket mice and
mountain beavers from the nearctic list, giving a conservative
estimate of sixty five per cent. From the palearctic, pandas, mole rats,
one family of jumping mice, pikas and the seleveniid mice, which were
only discovered in 1938, can be removed, giving the adjusted proportion, fifty eight per cent. Colugos, tree shrews, lorises, tarsiers,
tapirs, bamboo rats, spiny dormice and great apes, similarly, go from
the oriental total to give a forty eight per cent representation. The
ethiopian must lose otter shrews, golden moles, elephant shrews,
lorises, anomalurid squirrels, bamboo rats, spring haas and four other
rodent families to reduce the total, but still to give the lowest proportion of map fauna, forty six per cent.

It might seem from this analysis that the cartographers were a
poor second to the naturalists but this is not a justifiable conclusion
when some of the details are considered.

Many of the maps of the early sixteenth century, particularly those
showing the New World were, in fact, in advance of the contemporary
bestiaries. Although Oviedo had written a natural history of South
America by 1535 (Eden 1555) and had described armadillos, sloths
and anteaters; none of these animals was included in the first edition
of Gesner in 1551. But armadillos had already figured on Ribeiro's
world map of 1529 and Desceliers' world map of 1546. It is not until
1555 that an armadillo is recognised by a naturalist, in *Les observations
de plusieurs singularités et choses mémorables* by Belon. An anteater
reached Le Testu's map in 1566, Topsell's bestiary in 1607. Pictures
of sloths do not occur in the naturalists' books nor on maps.

Opossums, peccaries, llamas, several neotropical rodents, rheas,
macaws and iguanas had all figured on maps before 1551 and yet, by
then, only the opossum had attained the status of a bestiary animal.
Peccaries were admitted to Topsell's 1658 observations on the fauna

of America, guinea pigs had been admitted to his earlier work of 1607 and late editions of Gesner, but there is no sign of the other South American rodents, no sign of the llamas, rheas or definite macaws. An anteater was depicted in 1566 by Le Testu and by many subsequent mapmakers but arrived in Gesner's work only in later editions and in Topsell 1607. It seems likely that the anteater was copied from the cartographers unless they both had an as yet un-identified source. Anteating animals were, in general, ignored by the naturalists in spite of the fact that they had been much written about by the classical writers. Von Cube, in *Ortus Sanitatis* 1491, ventures formica maiones but, it seems, cartographers had fewer inhibitions and, probably, four different ones are represented: ratels, aardvark, pangolin and South American anteater.

Accurate giraffes were figured early on maps of the ethiopian region. The giraffe of the Genoese world map 1457 precedes von Breydenbach's admirable 1488 woodcut and is a considerably better representation of the animal than the fluffy camelopardalis in von Cube.

The achievement of the cartographers compared with the bestiary makers is further accentuated by finding that Gesner, in 1551, used an only slightly modified version of Olaus Magnus's 1539 lynxes and referred to Olaus Magnus as the authority. In later editions, Olaus Magnus's 1539 glutton appears, with acknowledgement but, like the lynxes, facing in the opposite direction from the map animals.

In contrast, turkeys arrived almost simultaneously on maps and in bestiaries. Desceliers had a turkey in the margin of his world map of 1550 at the latitude of Mexico and the following year an elegant but different turkey appeared in Gesner. Four years later, the well known Belon turkeys were published in *L'histoire de la nature des oyseaux* 1555. The comparisons are interesting. The three drawings are all adequate but different; but once again the cartographers showed themselves superior to the naturalists. Desceliers' turkey was situated in the nearctic but neither Gesner nor Belon were aware that it was a New World bird. Gesner quotes from the classical writers who were almost certainly describing the guinea fowl but maintains that his turkey came from India and was not a peacock but a fowl. Belon discusses the problem of whether the older writers really knew the turkey and concludes that they were describing the guinea fowl; but goes on to say that the turkey is little different from

o

Fig 10.1 Ribeiro's map of the
world 1529 in the Biblioteca
Vaticana: some mammals or birds in
all regions except the australian;
the neotropical and ethiopian faunas
are particularly abundant

this. It seems certain that Belon's turkeys were drawn from nearctic
specimens but he was evidently unaware that they had come from the
New World.

Information did not, however, always reach the cartographers
first. In 1551, Gesner forestalled the mapmakers by fifteen years with
a bird of paradise. Although not first to draw an armadillo, Belon
provided the original one that appeared on Le Testu's world map
of 1566. Gesner's or von Breydenbach's giraffe illustrated Prunes'
maps of 1559 and 1586.

The early bestiaries pre-date the animals of existing maps of the
thirteenth century. Thus, the twelfth and early thirteenth century
bestiaries have most of the animals that are represented on the
Ebstorf and Hereford maps although these animals evidently have
not been copied directly from any one bestiary. But, once again,
a mapmaker is ahead of the bestiaries with a camelopardalis in the
ethiopian region of the Ebstorf map. Camelopardalis does not
occur in the twelfth or the thirteenth century MS bestiaries but, in

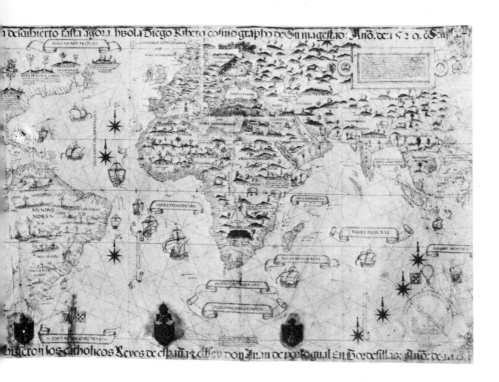

form no more accurate than the Ebstorf camelopardalis, it finds a place in von Cube.

The conclusion must be that while the early naturalists and cartographers compiled their bestiaries and maps mainly from the writings of Aristotle, Pliny, Aelian, Solinus and Isidore of Seville, cartographers of later centuries were no longer relying on these sources.

The naturalists abandoned the classical sources much more slowly. While Belon was debating whether the *Meleagris* of the ancients referred to a turkey or a guinea fowl, Desceliers was drawing a turkey in the nearctic region on the basis of reports from French explorers to America. Linschoten, who had translated Acosta's natural history into Dutch, introduced a definite tapir on his South American maps. Whereas some nine new South American mammals had occurred on the maps by the middle of the sixteenth century, there were only two South American mammals in the 1551 edition of Gesner, the opossum and the marmoset. The description of the opossum by Pinzon seems to have been the source for mapmakers and naturalists alike.

The cartographers show up well both in knowledge of new animals and in knowledge of the location of the animals. Their understanding of the geographical distribution of animals was so superior to that of the bestiary makers that the errors in placing of some animals hardly merit consideration. Blaeu's South American turkey is no more an error than Gesner's Indian turkey. The lapse that put a giraffe in North America and another in South America is hardly more serious than the reappearance of a manticora in the 1607 edition of Topsell. The cartographers' rare mistakes in animal location can be compared with their mistakes in land formation at the time. The continual appearance of unicorns seems to be based on the same sort of misunderstanding as the misinterpretation of Marco Polo's continental province of Indo-China, that turned it into a vast southern continent south of the Indian and Pacific Oceans to persist from Mercator's world chart of 1569 through two hundred years of map-making (Skelton 1958). That a map fauna of the australian region did not take shape is a reflection of the delay in discovering whether it existed.

A closer and more serious study of the work of the cartographers by some of their contemporary and later naturalists would have been a rewarding occupation. The information lying on these maps was slow to gain recognition. The portrayal of new animals on maps sometimes led to later copying into the bestiaries and natural histories. But the information about the distribution of the terrestrial mammals of the world was totally neglected. By the time the clue to the problem had been found, evolution, the unheeded information of the maps was outdated. As far as is known they were of no direct help to any zoogeographers though whether it was looking at the maps or reading journals that precipitated the questions of Thomas Browne and Robert Burton is not known. Had the maps been studied they would have been useful and certainly not misleading if zoological theory had progressed as fast as zoological and geographical practical knowledge.

Today, a zoologist cannot agree with the geographer who can write: 'The first real maps . . . were usually drawn by monastic scribes, who brought the skill with pen, brush and colours which they had acquired in illustrating manuscripts to portray a world in which scriptural teaching, classical and medieval myths, travellers' tales and the unnatural zoology of the Bestiaries were indiscriminately blended' (Lynam 1953).

REFERENCES

Acosta, J. d' 1589 *Historia natural y moral de las Indias* Leon
Acosta, J. d' 1604 *The Natural and Moral History of the Indies* London
Aelian about 200 *De Natura Animalium*, see A. F. Schofield 1958
Albertus Magnus 1240 *De Animalibus,* see H. Balss 1947
Albertus Magnus 1637 *The Secrets of Albertus Magnus* London
Aldrovandi, U. 1616 *De Quadrupedibus Solidipedibus*
Aldrovandi, U. 1621 *De Quadrupedibus Bisulcis*
Allardt, C. 1710 *Atlas Major* Amsterdam
Allardt, H. 1665 *Novii Belgi Novaeque Angliae* Amsterdam
Almagià, R. (ed) 1948 *Monumenta Cartographica Vaticana* Vatican City
Alvares, F. 1540 *Verdadera Informaçam dos terras do Preste Joam dos Indias*
    Lisbon
Amherst, Lord & Thomson, B. 1901 The Discovery of the Solomon Islands
    by Alvaro de Mendana *Hakluyt Soc. 2nd ser.* 7 & 8
Anville, J. B. B. d' 1737 *Nouvel Atlas de la Chine* The Hague
Apian, P. & Frison, G. 1544 *La Cosmographie* Antwerp
Apian, P. & Frison, G. 1584 *La Cosmographie* Antwerp
Arambourg, C. 1964 *Continental Vertebrate Faunas of the Tertiary of North
    Africa* London
Aristotle *De Caelo,* see J. L. Stocks 1930
Aristotle about 340 BC *Historia Animalium*, see d'Arcy W. Thompson 1910
Augustine of Hippo 412–427 *De Civitate Dei*, see J. H. 1610

Bagrow, L. 1951 *Die Geschichte der Kartographie* Berlin
Bagrow, L. 1959 Fragments of the 'Carta Marina' by L. Fries 1524 *Imago
    Mundi* 14, 111
Bagrow, L. & Skelton, R. A. 1964 *History of Cartography* London
Balss, H. 1947 *Albertus Magnus* Stuttgart
Barlow, R. 1540–1541 *A Brief Summe of Geographie*, see E. G. R. Taylor 1931
Barnikel, M. 1747 *Ducatus Curlandiae* Paris
Beaglehole, J. C. (ed) 1955 *The Journals of Captain James Cook on his Voyages
    of Discovery* Cambridge

Beckingham, C. F. & Huntingford, G. W. B. 1961–1962 A True Relation of the Lands of Prestor John by Father Francisco Alvares *Hakluyt Soc. 2nd ser.* 114 & 115

Belon, P. 1555a *Les observations de plusieurs singularitez et choses mémorables, trouvées en Grèce, Asie, Indée, Egypte, Arabie et autres pays étranges* Paris

Belon, P. 1555b *L'histoire de la nature des Oyseaux* Paris

Belon, P. 1557 *Portraits d'oyseaux, animaux, serpens, herbes, arbres, hommes et femmes d'Arabie et Egypte* Paris

Bestiarium, 12th century. British Museum *MS ADD 11283*

Bestiarium sive liber de natura animalium, 12th–13th century British Museum *MS Royal* 12 F *xiii*

Bestiary, 12th century. Bodleian Library Oxford *MS Bodley 764*

Biggar, H. P. 1924 The Voyages of Jacques Cartier *Public Archives of Canada* 11

Blaeu, W. J. 1630 *Appendix Theatri A. Ortelii et Atlantis G. Mercatoris* Amsterdam

Blaeu, W. J. 1643–1656 *Le théâtre du monde, ou nouvel atlas* Amsterdam

Blaeu, W. J. & G. 1635 *Theatrum Orbis Terrarum* Amsterdam

Blumer, W. 1964 The oldest known plan of an inhabited site dating from the Bronze Age about the middle of the 2nd millenium BC *Imago Mundi* 18, 9

Blundeville, T. 1594 *Exercises, Containing Eight Treatises* London

Bodenheimer, F. S. & Rabinowitz, A. 1948 *Timotheos of Gaza on Animals* Paris

Breydenbach, B. von 1488 *Exotische Tiere* Augsburg

Breydenbach, B. von 1488 *Reise ins heilige Land* Augsburg

Brion, M. 1959 *Animals in Art* London

Brouilette, B. 1934 *La chasse des animaux à fourrure au Canada* Paris

Browne, T. 1635 *Religio Medici* London

Bry, T. de 1590–1634 *America* Frankfurt-am-Main

Buffon, G. L. L. 1749–1804 *Histoire naturelle* Paris

Bure, A. 1626 *Orbis Arctôi* Amsterdam

Burnell, A. C. & Tiele, P. A. 1885 The Voyage of John Huyghen van Linschoten to the East Indies *Hakluyt Soc.* 70 & 71

Burney, J. 1803–1817 *A Chronological History of the Discoveries in the South Sea or Pacific Ocean* London

Burton, M. 1962 *Systematic Dictionary of Mammals of the World* London

Burton, R. 1628 *Anatomy of Melancholy* Oxford

Calaby, J. H. 1965 Early European description of an Australian mammal *Nature, Lond.* 205, 517

Camocio, G. F. 1933 *A large world map dated 1569* Philadelphia

Camöens, L. de 1572 *Os Lusiadas* Lisbon

Caraci, G. 1927 *Tabulae Geographicae Vetustiones in Italia Adservatae vol 2* Florence

Carletti, F. 1965 *My Voyage Round the World* London

Cartier, J. 1534–1541 *Voyages*, see H. P. Biggar 1924

Clark, W. E. le Gros 1959 *The Antecedents of Man* Edinburgh

Colbert, E. H. 1955 *Evolution of the Vertebrates* New York

Coote, C. H. (ed) 1895 *Remarkable Maps vol 2 & 3* Amsterdam

Coronelli, V. M. 1691–1696 *Atlante Veneto 4 vols* Venice

Cortesão, A. 1944 Suma Oriental of Tomé Pires 1512–1515, The Book of Francisco Rodriques *ca* 1515 *Hakluyt Soc. 2nd ser.* 89 & 90

Cortesão, A. 1954 *The Nautical Chart of 1424* Coimbra

Cortesão, A. & Texeira da Mota, A. (eds) 1960 *Portugaliae Monumenta Cartographica* Lisbon

Creer, K. M. 1964 Palaeomagnetic data and du Toit's reconstruction of Gondwanaland *Nature, Lond.* 204, 369

Crescentius, P. 1538 *De Omnibus Agriculturae Partibus* Basel

Crone, G. R. 1937 The Voyages of Cadamosto *Hakluyt Soc. 2nd ser.* 80

Crone, G. R. 1953 *Maps and their Makers* London

Crone, G. R. 1954 *World Map of Richard of Haldingham* London

Crowley, F. J., Crow, J. A., Pasinetti, P. M. & Sobel, E. 1959 Semeiança del mundo *Univ. Calif. Publ. Mod. Philol.* 51

Cube, J. von 1491 *Ortus Sanitatis* Mainz

Curnow, L. J. 1930 *The World Mapped* London

Cuvier, G. 1799 Mémoire sur les espèces d'éléphans vivantes et fossiles *Mém. de l'Institut (Class. Math. Phys.)* 2, 1

Cuvier, G. 1817 *Le règne animal* Paris

Cuvier, G. 1827 *The animal Kingdom* London

Dampier, W. 1697 *A New Voyage Round the World* London

Dampier, W. 1703 *A Voyage to New Holland, etc. In the year 1699* London

Darlington, P. J. 1957 *Zoogeography: The Geographical Distribution of Animals* New York

Darlington, P. J. 1965 *Biogeography of the Southern End of the World* Cambridge, Mass.

Darlington, W. 1849 *Memorials of John Bartram and Humphry Marshall* Philadelphia

Darwin, C. 1859 *On the Origin of Species by Means of Natural Selection* London

Delacour, J. & Mayr, E. 1945 The family Anatidae *Wilson Bull.* 57, 3

Delaunay, P. 1962 *La Zoologie au seizième siècle* Paris

Druce, G. C. 1923 An account of the 'mirmecoleon' or Ant-lion *Antiquaries J.* 3, 347

Druce, G. C. 1936 *The Bestiary of Guillaume Le Clerc* Ashford

Eden, R. 1555 *The History of Travayle in the West and East Indies* London

Edwards, H. Milne 1868–1874 *Recherches pour servir à l'histoire naturelle des mammiferes comprenant des considérations sur la classification de ces animaux* Paris

Ellerman, J. R. 1940 *The Families and Genera of Living Rodents* London

Ellerman, J. R. & Morrison-Scott, T. C. S. 1951 *Check List of Palearctic and Indian Mammals 1758 to 1946* London

Enciso, M. F. de 1518 *Suma de Geographia* Seville, see E. G. R. Taylor 1931

Fanshawe, R. (trans) 1655 *The Lusiad* London
Fonteneau, J. 1544 *La Cosmographie* see G. Musset 1904
Forlani, P. di 1565 *Universale Descriptione di Tutta la Terra* Venice
Franciscum, J. 1557 *Palestinae sive Terrae Sanctae Descriptio* Rome
Franklin, B. 1786 A letter from Dr. Benjamin Franklin to Mr. Alphonse le Roy *Trans. Amer. Phil. Soc. Philad.* 2, 294

Gadow, H. 1901 *Amphibia and Reptiles* London
Galvano, A. 1601 *Booke of the Discoveries of the World,* see J. Burney 1803–1817 and S. Purchas 1625
Gastaldi, J. 1550 *L'Universale Orbe della Terra* Venice
George, W. 1962 *Animal Geography* London
George, W. 1964a *Biologist Philosopher: A Study of the Life and Writings of Alfred Russel Wallace* London
George, W. 1964b Use of biogeography in authenticating early discoveries *Geogr. J.* 130, 315
George, W. 1964c An early European description of an Australasian Mammal *Nature, Lond.* 202, 1130
George, W. 1965 Early European description of an Australian Mammal *Nature, Lond.* 205, 517
George, W. 1968 The Yale *J. Warburg and Courtauld Inst.* 31, 423
Gesner, C. 1551 *Historiae Animalium* Zurich
Gesner, C. 1585 *Historiae Animalium III De Avibus* Frankfurt-am-Main
Gesner, C. 1620 *Historiae Animalium* Frankfurt-am-Main
Gilliard, E. T. 1958 *Living Birds of the World* London
Giraldi, A. 1954–1955 *Amerigo Vespucci* Florence
Golding, A. 1590 *Polyhistor* London
Golding, A. 1590 *The Situation of the World by Pomponius Mela* London
Goldsmith, O. 1776 *An History of the Earth and Animated Nature* Dublin
Grande, S. 1905 *Le Carte d'America di Giacomo Gastaldi* Turin
Greenlee, W. B. 1938 The Voyage of Pedro Alvares Cabral to Brazil and India 1500 *Hakluyt Soc. 2nd ser.* 81

H., J (trans) 1610 *Augustine of Hippo De Civitate Dei* London
Hakluyt, R. 1598–1600 *The Principal Navigations Voyages Traffiques and Discoveries of the English Nation* London
Hall, E. R. & Kelson, K. R. 1959 *The Mammals of North America* New York
Harlan, R. 1825 *Fauna Americana* Philadelphia
Harrington, H. J. 1962 Paleogeographic development of South America *Bull. Amer. Ass. Petroleum Geol.* 46, 1773
Heawood, E. 1927 *A map of the world on Mercator's projection by Jodocus Hondius Amsterdam 1608 from the unique copy in the collection of the Royal Geographical Society* London
Heawood, E. 1943 An unrecorded Blaeu world map of *ca* 1618 *Geogr. J.* 102, 170
Herodotus *The Histories,* see A. de Sélincourt 1954

Hervé, M. R. 1955 Australia in French geographical documents of the renaissance *J. Roy. Austral. Historical Soc.* 41, 23

Hondius, J. 1608 *A map of the world on Mercator's projection,* see E. Heawood 1927

Hop, H. 1778 *Nouvelle description du Cap de Bonne-Espérance* Amsterdam

Isidorus, Bishop of Seville 1493 *Ethimologiarum libri viginti* Venice

James, M. R. 1929 *Marvels of the East* Oxford

Jane, C. 1930–1933 Select Documents illustrating the four Voyages of Colombus *Hakluyt Soc. 2nd ser.* 65 & 70

Janssonius, J. 1646 *Novus Atlas* Amsterdam

Jefferys, T. 1776 *The American Atlas* London

Jode, G. de 1578 *Speculum Orbis Terrae* Antwerp

Jode, G. de 1593 *Speculum Orbis Terrae* Antwerp

Johnston, A. K. 1848 *The Physical Atlas of Natural Phenomena* London

Jomard, E. F. 1854–1862 *Les monuments de la géographie* Paris

Jones, G. 1961 *Eirik the Red and other Icelandic Sagas* Oxford

Jones, H. L. 1917 *The Geography of Strabo* London

Justel, H. 1674 *Recueil de divers voyages* Paris

Kahle, P. 1956 *Opera Minora* Leyden

Kammerer, A. 1935 *La Mer Rouge, l'Assyrie et l'Arabie* Cairo

Keller, O. 1909 *Die Antike Tierwelt* Leipzig

Keulen, J. van 1660 *Nova Tabula Terrarum* Amsterdam

Keulen, J. van 1682 *De Zee-Atlas* Amsterdam

Kimble, G. H. T. 1937 Esmeraldo de Situ Orbis *Hakluyt Soc. 2nd ser.* 79

Kitchin, T. 1794 *A New Universal Atlas* London

Koeman, C. 1952 *Tabulae Geographicae quibus Colonia Bonae Spei Antiqua Depingitur* Amsterdam

Le Testu, G. 1555 *Cosmographie Universelle* MS Paris

Letts, M. 1953 Mandeville's Travels: Texts and Translations *Hakluyt Soc.* 101 & 102

Levaillant, F. 1806 *Histoire naturelle des oiseaux de paradis et des rolliers* Paris

Levillier, R. 1948 *America la bien llamada* Buenos Aires

Levillier, R. 1951 *Amerigo Vespucci El Nuevo Mundo* Buenos Aires

Lhote, H. 1959 *Tassili Frescoes* London

Linnaeus, C. 1758 *Systema Naturae* Stockholm

Linschoten, J. H. van 1594–1605 *Itinerario* Amsterdam

Linschoten, J. H. van 1598 *Discours of Voyages into ye Easte and West Indies* London

Lyell, C. 1830–1833 *Principles of Geology* London

Lynam, E. 1949 *The Carta Marina of Olaus Magnus, Venice 1539 and Rome 1572* Jenkintown, Penn.

Lynam, E. 1953 *The Mapmaker's Art* London

McCrindle, J. W. 1882 *Ancient India as described by Ktêsias the Knidian* Calcutta

McDowell, S. 1948 The bony palate of birds: the Palaeognathae *Auk* 65, 520

Magnus, O. 1539 *Opera Breve* Venice

Magnus, O. 1555 *Historia de Gentibus Septentrionalibus* Rome

Magnus, O. 1658 *A Compendious History of the Goths, Swedes and Vandals and other Northern Nations* London

Mair, A. W. 1958 *Oppian's Cynegetica* London & Cambridge, Mass.

Marcel, G. 1896 *Choix de cartes des XIV et XV siècles* Paris

Margry, P. 1867 *Les navigations françaises et la révolution maritime du XIV au XVI siècle* Paris

Markham, C. R. 1859 Narrative of the Embassy of Ruy Gonzalez de Clavijo to the Court of Timour, at Samarcan AD 1403–1406 *Hakluyt Soc.* 26

Markham, C. R. 1893 The Journal of Christopher Columbus (during his first voyage 1492–1493) and Documents Relating to the Voyages of John Cabot and Gaspar Corte Real *Hakluyt Soc* 86

Markham, C. R. 1911 Early Spanish Voyages to the Straits of Magellan *Hakluyt Soc. 2nd ser.* 28

Marlow, B. J. 1965 Early European description of an Australian mammal *Nature, Lond.* 205, 516

Martieri, P. 1516–1530 *De Orbe Novo Decades,* see R. Eden 1555

Matthew, W. D. 1915 Climate and evolution *Ann. N. Y. Acad. Sci.* 24, 171

Megenburg, K. von 1491 *Das Buch der Natur* Augsburg

Mela, P. about 43 *De Situ Orbis,* see A. Golding 1590

Mercator, G. 1578 *Tabulae Geographicae Cl. Ptolemei* Cologne

Mercator, G. 1875 *Sphère terrestre et sphère céleste de Gérard Mercator* Brussels

Mercator, G. & Hondius, J. 1606 *Atlas sive Cosmographicae Meditationes de Fabrica Mundi et Fabricati Figura* Amsterdam

Mercator, G. & Hondius, J. 1636 *The Newe Atlas* Amsterdam

Miller, K. 1895a *Die Ältesten Welkarten* Stuttgart

Miller, K. 1895b *Ebstorfkarte* Stuttgart

Moll, H. 1723 *The Compleat Geographer or Moll's Geography* London

Morden, R. 1680 *Map of the English Empire in the Continent of America* Bodleian Library Oxford *MS Ashmole* 1820b

Moreau, R. E. 1952 Africa since the Mesozoic *Proc. Zool. Soc. Lond.* 21, 869

Müller, C. 1855 *Geographi Graeci Minores* Paris

Münster, S. & Belle Forest, F. 1575 *La cosmographie universelle de tout le monde* Paris

Musset, G. 1904 *La cosmographie par Jean Fonteneau dit Alfonse de Saintonge* Paris

Nordenskiöld, A. E. 1889 *Facsimile Atlas to the Early History of Cartography* Stockholm

Nordenskiöld, A. E. 1897 *Periplus* Stockholm

Nørlund, N. E. 1944 *Islands Kortlaegning* Copenhagen

Nunn, G. E. 1934 *The Mappemonde of Juan de la Cosa: a Critical Investigation of its Date* Jenkintown, Penn.

Oberhummer, E. 1924 *Die Welkarte des P. Desceliers, von 1553* Vienna
Ogilby, J. 1671 *America* London
Oppian about 212 *Cynegetica*, see A. W. Mair 1958
Ortelius, A. 1590 *Theatrum Orbis* Antwerp
Oviedo, G. F. about 1535 *Summarie of the Generall Hystorie of the West Indies*, see R. Eden 1555 & G. B. Ramusio 1557

Pasterot, Pilote 1587 *Livre de la marine* British Museum *Egerton MS* 1513
Pausanias about 174 *Graeciae Descriptio*, see T. Taylor 1824
Pelseneer, P. 1904 La 'Ligne de Weber' limite zoologique de l'Asie et de l'Australie *Bull. Acad. Roy. Belg. Cl. Sci.* 1001
Pennant, T. 1791 *Indian Zoology* London
Penzer, N. M. 1937 *The Most Noble and Famous Travels of Marco Polo together with the Travels of Nicolo de Conti edited from the Elizabethan Translation of John Frampton* London
Pereira, D. P. 1505–1508 *Esmeraldo de Situ Orbis*, see G. H. T. Kimble 1937
Pigafetta, A. 1525 *Navigation et descouvrement de la Indie supérieure*, see J. A. Robertson 1906 & Stanley of Alderley 1874
Pilgrim, G. E. 1941 The dispersal of the Artiodactyla *Biol. Rev.* 16
Pires, T. 1512–1515 *Suma Oriental*, see A. Cortesão 1944
Pliny about 77–79 *Naturalis Historia*, see H. Rackham 1940
Polo, M. 1298 *Travels*, see H. Yule & H. Cordier 1903
Porcacchi, T. 1572 *L'Isole piu Famose del Mondo* Venice
Prado y Tovar, D. de 1608 *Relación*, see H. N. Stevens & G. F. Barwick 1930
Purchas, S. 1625 *Hakluytus Posthumus or Purchas His Pilgrimes* London

Rackham, H. 1940 *Pliny Natural History* London & Cambridge, Mass.
Radinsky, L. B. 1965 Early tertiary Tapiroidea of Asia *Bull. Amer. Mus. Nat. Hist.* 129, 181
Raffles, T. S. 1821 Descriptive catalogue of a zoological collection made on account of the Honourable East India Company in the Island of Sumatra and its vicinity *Trans. Linn. Soc. Lond.* 13, 239
Raisz, E. 1948 *General Cartography* New York
Ramusio, G. B. 1557 *Delle Navigatione et Viaggi* Venice
Ravenstein, E. G. 1898 A Journal of the First Voyage of Vasco da Gama 1497–1499 *Hakluyt Soc.* 99
Ravenstein, E. G. 1908 *Martin Behaim: His Life and His Globe* London
Re'is, P. 1513 *Map of the World*, see P. Kahle 1956
Robertson, J. A. 1906 *Magellan's Voyage Around the World by Antonio Pigafetta* Cleveland
Rockhil, W. W. 1900 The Journey of William of Rubruck to the Eastern Parts of the World 1253–1255 *Hakluyt Soc. 2nd ser.* 4
Runcorn, S. K. (ed) 1962 *Continental Drift* New York

Sanderson, I. T. 1955 *Living Mammals of the World* London
Santa Cruz, A. de 1540 *Islario General de Todas las Islas del Mundo*, see K. R. von Wieser 1908

Santarem, le vicomte de 1849 *Atlas composé de mappemondes, de portolans et de cartes hydrographiques et historiques* Paris
Schoff, W. H. 1912 *The Periplus of the Erythraean Sea* New York
Schofield, A. F. 1958–1959 *Aelian on the Characteristics of Animals* London & Cambridge Mass.
Sclater, P. L. 1858 On the general distribution of the members of the class Aves *J. Linn. Soc.* 2, 130
Sélincourt, A. de 1954 *Herodotus the Histories* London
Seller, J. 1671 *The English Pilot* London
Sharp, A. 1963 *The Discovery of Australia* Oxford
Shepard, O. 1930 *The Lore of the Unicorn* London
Simpson, G. G. 1940 Antarctica as a faunal migration route *Proc. 6th. Pacific Sci. Congr.* 2, 755
Simpson, G. G. 1945 The principles of classification and a classification of the mammals *Bull. Amer. Mus. Nat. Hist.* 85, 1
Simpson, G. G. 1947 Holarctic faunas *Bull. Geol. Soc. Amer.* 58, 613
Simpson, G. G. 1950 History of the fauna of Latin America *Amer. Scientist* 38, 361
Simpson, G. G. 1953 *Evolution and Geography* Eugene, Oregon
Simpson, G. G. 1961 Historical zoogeography of Australian mammals *Evolution* 15, 431
Skelton, R. A. 1952 *Decorative Printed Maps of the 15th to 16th Centuries* London
Skelton, R. A. 1958 *Explorers' Maps* London
Skelton, R. A., Marston, T. E. & Painter, G. D. 1965 *The Vinland Map and the Tartar Relation* New Haven
Smith, S. 1928 *Early History of Assyria* London
Solinus, J. *Polyhistor*, see A. Golding 1590
Speed, J. 1631 *A Prospect of the Most Famous Parts of the World* London
Speed, J. 1646 *Theatre of the Empire of Great Britain* London
Speed, J. 1676 *Theatre of the Empire of Great Britain together with a prospect of the most Famous Parts of the World* London
Stanley of Alderley 1874 The First Voyage Round the World by Magellan *Hakluyt Soc.* 52
Stevens, H. N. & Barwick, G. F. 1930 New Light on the Discovery of Australia as revealed by the Journal of Captain Don Diego de Prado y Tovar *Hakluyt Soc. 2nd ser.* 64
Stocks, J. L. 1930 *Aristotle De Caelo* Oxford
Strabo 7 BC–AD 19 *Geography*, see H. L. Jones 1917
Swift, J. 1733 *On Poetry: A Rapsody* London

Taylor, E. G. R. 1931 A Brief Summe of Geographie by Roger Barlow 1540–1541 *Hakluyt Soc. 2nd ser.* 69
Taylor, T. 1824 *The Description of Greece by Pausanias* London
Termier, H. & Termier, G. 1960 *Atlas de paléogéographie* Paris
Thompson, D'Arcy W. 1910 *Aristotle Historia Animalium* Oxford

Timotheos of Gaza about 100 *On Animals*, see F. S. Bodenheimer & A. Rabinowitz 1948

Toit, A. L. du 1937 *Our Wandering Continents* Edinburgh

Tooley, R. V. 1949 *Maps and Map-makers* London

Topsell, E. 1607 *The Historie of Foure-Footed Beastes* London

Topsell, E. 1658 *The History of Four-footed Beasts and Serpents and Insects* London

Troughton, E. 1941 *The Furred Animals of Australia* Sydney

Umbgrove, J. H. F. 1949 *Structural History of the East Indies* Cambridge

Unger, E. 1937 From the cosmos picture to the world map *Imago Mundi* 2, 1

Urdaneta, A. de about 1537 *Narrative of the Voyage Undertaken to the Malucas or Spice Islands by the Fleet Commanded by the Comendador Garcia Jofre de Loaysa,* see C. R. Markham 1911

Valk, G. 1690 *A collection of maps of the world by Gerard Valk* Amsterdam

Vespucci, A. 1500–1504 *Mundus Novus and Other Letters,* see R. Levillier 1951

Vincent de Beauvais 1591 *Speculi Maioris Tomi Quator Naturalis Historiae* Venice

Vindel, F. 1955–1959 *Mapas de América en los Libros Españoles de los Siglos XVI al XVII (1503–1798)* Madrid

Visscher, N. J. 1655 *Novi Belgii Novaeque Anglae nec non Partis Virginiae Tabula* Amsterdam

Waghenaer, L. J. 1588 *The Mariner's Mirror* London

Waghenaer, L. J. 1588 *Spieghel der Zeevaerdt* Leyden

Waghenaer, L. J. 1596 *Den Nieuwen Spieghel der Zeevaert* Amsterdam

Wagner, H. R. 1951 A map of Sancho Gutiérrez of 1551 *Imago Mundi* 8, 47

Wallace, A. R. 1863 On the physical geography of the Malay Archipelago *J. Geogr. Soc.* 33, 217

Wallace, A. R. 1864 On the parrots of the Malayan region with remarks on their habits, distribution and affinities and the descriptions of two new species *Proc. Zool. Soc. Lond.* 272

Wallace, A. R. 1869 *The Malay Archipelago* London

Wallace, A. R. 1876 *The Geographical Distribution of Animals* London

Wallace, A. R. 1910 *The World of Life* London

Weber, M. 1902 *Der Indo-Australische Archipel und die Geschichte seiner Tierwelt* Jena

Wells, E. 1701 *A New Sett of Maps both of Antient and Present Geography Together with a Geographical Treatise* Oxford

Wieder, F. C. 1925–1933 *Monumenta Cartographica* The Hague

Wieser, K. R. von 1908 *Die Karte von Amerika in dem Islario General de Alonso de Santa Cruz* Innsbruck

Williamson, J. A. 1962 The Cabot Voyages and Bristol Discovery under Henry VII *Hakluyt Soc. 2nd ser.* 120

Winter, H. 1950 A late portolan chart at Madrid and late portolan charts in general *Imago Mundi* 7, 37

Wittkower, R. 1942 Marvels of the East. A study in the history of monsters *J. Warburg & Courtauld Institutes* 5, 159

Wood, A. E. 1950 Porcupines, paleogeography and parallelism *Evolution* 4, 87

Wood, C. A. & Fyfe, F. M. 1943 *The Art of Falconry being the De Arte Venandi cum Avibus of Frederick II of Hohenstaufen* Stanford

Wotton, E. 1552 *De Differentiis Animalium* Paris

Wytfliet, C. 1605 *Histoire universelle des Indes orientales et occidentales* Douay

Youssouf Kamal, Prince 1926–1951 *Monumenta Cartographica Africae et Aegypti* Cairo

Yule, H. 1866 Cathay and the Way Thither *Hakluyt Soc* 36 & 37

Yule, H. & Cordier, H. 1903 *The Book of Ser Marco Polo (the Venetian)* London

Yule, H. & Cordier, H. 1915 Cathay and the Way Thither *Hakluyt Soc. 2nd ser.* 33, 37, 38 & 41

Yusuf Akçura 1935 *Piri Reis Haritasi* Istanbul

Zeuner, F. E. 1963 *A History of Domesticated Animals* London

INDEX

Date Due

JAN 16 '71

JAN 19 '72

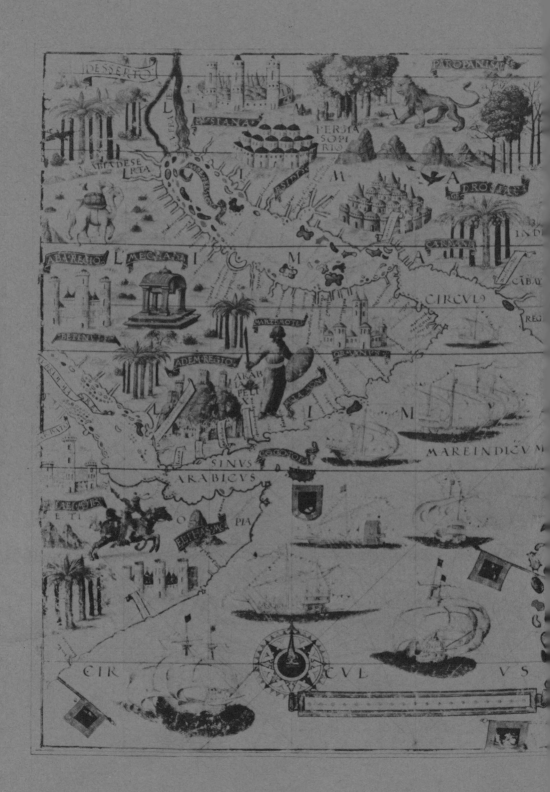